Rick Steves'
SNAPSHOT

Milan & the Italian Lakes District

CONTENTS

INTRODUCTION

This Snapshot guide, excerpted from my guidebook *Rick Steves' Italy*, introduces you to Milan. If Florence represents the Renaissance and Rome equals antiquity, Milan is 21st-century Italy. You can walk on the rooftop of one of Europe's grandest Gothic cathedrals, window-shop in fashionable neighborhoods, visit the world's most famous opera house, and admire a Leonardo masterpiece. Explore the city's grand, glass-domed arcade and stroll along one of Europe's longest pedestrian-only boulevards. Sip an *aperitivo* at a sidewalk café, and sample Milan's culinary specialties. If you're looking for a sophisticated, smart slice of Italy, you'll find it here.

To help you have the best trip possible, I've included the following topics in this book.

• **Planning Your Time**, with advice on how to make the most of your limited time

• **Orientation,** including tourist information (abbreviated as TI), tips on public transportation, local tour options, and helpful hints

• **Sights** with ratings:

    ▲▲▲—Don't miss

    ▲▲—Try hard to see

    ▲—Worthwhile if you can make it

    No rating—Worth knowing about

• **Sleeping** and **Eating**, with good-value recommendations in every price range

• **Connections,** with tips on trains, buses, and driving

Practicalities, near the end of this book, has information on money, phoning, hotel reservations, transportation, and more, plus Italian survival phrases.

To travel smartly, read this little book in its entirety before you go. It's my hope that this guide will make your trip more meaningful and rewarding. Traveling like a temporary local, you'll get the absolute most out of every mile, minute, and dollar.

Buon viaggio!

Rick Steves

MILAN

Milano

For every church in Rome, there's a bank in Milan. Italy's second city and the capital of Lombardy, Milan is a hardworking, fashion-conscious, time-is-money city of 1.3 million. It's a melting pot of people and history. Milan's industriousness may come from the Teutonic blood of its original inhabitants, the Lombards, or from the region's Austrian heritage. Milan is Italy's fashion, industrial, banking, TV, publishing, and convention capital. The economic success of postwar Italy can be attributed, in part, to this city of publicists and pasta power lunches.

As if to make up for its rough, noisy big-city-ness, the Milanesi people are works of art. Milan is an international fashion capital with a refined taste. Window displays are gorgeous, cigarettes are chic, and even the cheese comes gift-wrapped. Yet thankfully, Milan is no more expensive for tourists than other Italian cities.

Three hundred years before Christ, the Romans called this place Mediolanum, or "the central place." By the fourth century A.D., it was the capital of the western half of the Roman Empire. Emperor Constantine issued the Edict of Milan from here, legalizing Christianity. After some barbarian darkness, medieval Milan became a successful mercantile city, eventually rising to regional prominence under the Visconti and Sforza families. By the time of the Renaissance, it was nicknamed "the New Athens," and was enough of a cultural center for Leonardo da Vinci to call it home. Then came 400 years of foreign domination (Spain, Austria, France, more Austria). Milan was a center of the 1848 revolution against Austria, and helped lead Italy to unification in 1870.

Mussolini left a heavy fascist touch on the architecture here (such as the central train station). His excesses also led to the

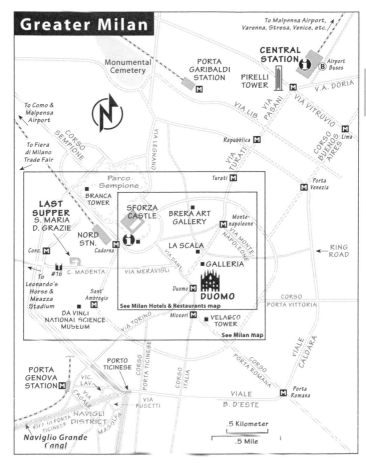

Greater Milan

To Malpensa Airport,
Varenna, Stresa, Venice, etc.

CENTRAL
STATION

PORTA
GARIBALDI
STATION

PIRELLI
TOWER

Airport
Buses

Monumental
Cemetery

V.A. DORIA

VIA LIB.

VIA PASANI

VIA VITRUVIO

To Como &
Malpensa
Airport

CORSO
SEMPIONE

VIA LEGNANO

Repubblica

VIA TURATI

CORSO
BUENOS
AIRES

Lima

To Fiera
di Milano
Trade Fair

Parco
Sempione

Turati

Porta
Venezia

BRANCA
TOWER

LAST
SUPPER
S. MARIA
D. GRAZIE

SFORZA
CASTLE

BRERA ART
GALLERY

Monte-
napoleone

VIA MONTE
NAPOLEONE

RING
ROAD

NORD
STN.

Conc.

Cadorna

LA SCALA

VIA DANTE

VIA MERAVIGLI

GALLERIA

#16

C. MAGENTA

To
Leonardo's
Horse &
Meazza
Stadium

Sant'
Ambrogio

Duomo

DUOMO

CORSO
PORTA VITTORIA

DA VINCI
NATIONAL SCIENCE
MUSEUM

VIA TORINO

Missori

VELASCO
TOWER

See Milan Hotels & Restaurants map

See Milan map

PORTA
GENOVA
STATION

PORTO
TICINESE

VIC.
LAV.

VIA
CASALE

CORSO
PORTA TICINESE

CORSO
ITALIA

PORTA
ROMANA

VIALE
CALDARA

VIA
FUSETTI

NAVIGLI
DISTRICT

VIA PORTA
TICINESE

MAZON

VIALE
B. D'ESTE

Porta
Romana

Naviglio Grande
Canal

.5 Kilometer

.5 Mile

MILAN

WWII bombing of Milan. But the city rose again. The 1959 Pirelli Tower (the skinny skyscraper in front of the station) was a trendsetter in its day. Today, Milan is people-friendly, with a great transit system and inviting pedestrian zones. And the city is busy with construction projects in an effort to beef up both its infrastructure and cultural offerings as it prepares to host the 2015 World's Fair in the Rho-Pero district. The area is revamping its layout with new parks, museums, and American-style skyscrapers to welcome the expected 20 million visitors. An estimated 130 to 150 countries will display exhibits about their contributions to sustainable development (for more information, see http://en.expo2015.org).

Many tourists come to Italy for the past. But Milan is today's Italy, and no trip to this country is complete without visiting it. While it's not big on the tourist circuit, the city has plenty to see.

MILAN

And fortunately, seeing Milan—so manageable and well-organized—is not difficult.

For pleasant excursions from the city, consider visiting Lake Como or Lake Maggiore—both are about an hour from Milan by train.

Planning Your Time

OK, it's a big, intense city, so you probably won't linger. Compared to Rome and Florence, Milan's art is mediocre, but the city does have unique and noteworthy sights: the Duomo and Galleria Vittorio Emanuele II, Pinacoteca Ambrosiana, La Scala Opera House, Brera Art Gallery, Michelangelo's last *Pietà* in Sforza Castle, and Leonardo's *Last Supper* (which is hard to see without making a reservation long in advance).

With two nights and a full day, you can gain an appreciation for the town and see the major sights. On a short visit, I'd focus on the center. Tour the Duomo, hit the art you like, browse through the elegant shopping area and the Galleria Vittorio Emanuele II, and try to see an opera. Technology buffs like the Leonardo da Vinci National Science and Technology Museum, while history and art buffs dig the city's early Christian  churches, Brera Gallery, Pinacoteca Ambrosiana, and Museo del Novecento. People-watchers and pigeon-feeders could spend their entire visit never losing sight of the Duomo. And if you dig burial grounds, rattle through Milan's evocative Monumental Cemetery. To maximize your time in Milan, use the Metro and note which places stay open through the siesta.

Since Milan is a cold Italian plunge, and most flights to the US leave Milan early in the morning, you could save it for the end of your trip and start your journey softly by going directly by train from Milan to Lake Como (one-hour ride to Varenna) or the Cinque Terre (3-4 hours to Monterosso). Then spend the last night or two of your trip in Milan before flying home.

Monday is a terrible sightseeing day, since many museums are closed (including the church that houses Leonardo's *Last Supper*). August is oppressively hot and muggy, and locals who can vacate at this time do, leaving the city pretty quiet. Those visiting in August find that the nightlife is sleepy and many shops and restaurants are closed. Some hotels are closed; other hotel rooms are on the discounted push list.

A Three-Hour Tour: If you're just changing trains in Milan's Centrale Station (as, sooner or later, you probably will), consider catching a later train and taking this blitz tour: Check your bag at the station, pick up a city map at the station TI, ride the subway to the Duomo, peruse the square, explore the cathedral's rooftop and interior, have a scenic coffee in the Galleria Vittorio Emanuele II, spin on the floor mosaic of the bull for good luck, see a museum or two (most are within a 10-minute walk of the main square), and return by subway to the station. Art fans could make time for *The Last Supper* (if they've made reservations), the Michelangelo *Pietà* in Sforza Castle (no reservations necessary), the Brera Art Gallery, or the Pinacoteca Ambrosiana (with its Leonardo exhibit).

Orientation to Milan

My coverage focuses on the old center. Most sights and hotels are within a 10-minute walk of the cathedral (Duomo), which is a straight eight-minute Metro ride from the central train station.

Tourist Information

Milan has two TIs: The main TI is at Piazza Castello 1 (near Sforza Castle), and the other is at the Milano Centrale train station, in front of track 13 (both share the same hours: Mon-Fri 9:00-17:00, Sat-Sun 9:00-12:30, main TI tel. 02-7740-4343, train station TI tel. 02-7740-4318, www.turismo.milano.it). You can book Autostradale and Zani Viaggi city tours (see "Tours in Milan," later) at the companies' offices on Piazza Castello, near the main TI.

I've listed enough sights to keep you very busy for two days, but there's much more to see in Milan. Its many thousand-year-old churches make it clear that Milan was an important beacon in the Dark Ages. The TI and local guidebooks can point you in the right direction if you have more time.

Arrival in Milan

By Train at Milano Centrale: The huge, sternly decorated, fascist-built (in 1931) central train station is a sight in itself. Recently cleaned, the halls feel more monumental than ever. Notice how the art makes you feel small—it emphasizes that a powerful state is a good thing. In the front lobby, heroic people celebrate "modern" transportation (circa-1930 ships, trains, and cars) opposite reliefs depicting old-fashioned sailboats and horse carts.

The station has three levels of **shops and services.** The WCs are by track 22 (€1, daily 6:00-24:00). Stepping out of the platform area and into the shopping corridor, you'll find the big neon-green cross of the 24-hour pharmacy to your left. If you ride the moving walkways down two more levels, you'll reach the **Trenitalia ticket office** (daily 5:50-22:20) and user-friendly ticket sales machines (gray-and-blue for local train services only, red-white-and-green

Rome vs. Milan: A Classic Squabble

In Italy, the North and South bicker about each other, hurling barbs, quips, and generalizations. All the classic North/South traits can be applied to Milan (the business capital) and Rome (the government and religious capital). People like to say that people come to Milan to sin and go to Rome to ask for forgiveness. Although the differences have become less pronounced lately, the sniping continues.

The Milanesi say the Romans are lazy. Roman government jobs come with short hours—cut even shorter by too many coffee breaks, three-hour lunches, chats with colleagues, and phone calls to friends and relatives. Milanesi contend that "Roma *ladrona*" (Rome, the big thief) is a parasite that lives off the taxes of people up North. There's still a strong Milan-based movement seriously promoting secession from the South.

Romans, meanwhile, dismiss the Milanesi as uptight workaholics with nothing else to live for—gray like their foggy city. Romans do admit that in Milan, job opportunities are better and based on merit. And the Milanesi grudgingly concede the Romans have a gift for enjoying life.

While Rome is more of a family city, Milan is the place for

for all Italian trains, credit cards and cash accepted, you can't buy international tickets from machines). Also on this level, you'll find taxis, travel agencies, shuttle buses to the airports, and a baggage check (marked *deposito bagagli*, €5/5 hours, €13/24 hours, 5-day maximum, daily 6:00-23:00, passport required, 45-pound bag limit). Just outside the front entrance of the station are car-rental offices and the Metro (clearly marked). An ATM is on the lower Metro level.

The **365 Travel Agency**—which sells train tickets, supplements, and night-train berth reservations—has three offices at the station. One is across from the baggage-check *deposito* desk (has longest hours, daily 7:00-21:00, agency tel. 02-6738-2603, www.agenzie365.it); another is outside facing the airport shuttle buses on Piazza Luigi di Savoia; and a third is on the opposite side of the station near the Sisley fashion store (with your back to the tracks, exit right). Their 7 percent commission can be a reasonable price to pay to skip the Trenitalia ticket lines.

Taking the Metro from Milano Centrale to the Duomo and Back: For a quick visit, it's a straight shot on the underground from Centrale Station to the Duomo: Buy a €1.50 ticket at a kiosk or

MILAN

high-powered singles on the career fast track. Milanese yuppies mix with each other...not the city's longtime residents. Milan is seen as wary of foreigners and inward-looking, and Rome as fun-loving, tolerant, and friendly. In Milan, bureaucracy (like social services) works logically and efficiently, while in Rome, accom-

plishing even small chores can be exasperating. Everything in Rome—from finding a baby-sitter to buying a car—is done through friends. Meanwhile, people in Milan are more private.

Milanesi find Romans vulgar. The Roman dialect is considered one of the coarsest in the country. Much as they try, Milanesi just can't say "Damn your dead relatives" quite as effectively as the Romans. Still, Milanesi enjoy Roman comedians and love to imitate the accent.

The Milanesi feel that Rome is dirty and Roman traffic nerve-wracking. But despite the craziness, Rome maintains a genuine village feel. People share family news with their neighborhood grocer. Milan lacks people-friendly piazzas, and entertainment comes at a high price. But in Rome, *la dolce vita* is as close as the nearest square, and a full moon is enjoyed by all.

from the machines, follow signs for yellow line 3 (direction: San Donato), and after an eight-minute ride (four stops), you'll be facing the cathedral. To return, ride the same yellow line 3 back the other way (direction: Comasina).

By Train at Milano Cadorna: You're most likely to use this humble little commuter railway station for its airport shuttle train. Malpensa Express generally uses track 1. The station has WCs, taxis, and handy eateries; the Cadorna Metro station is directly in front.

By Train at Milano Porta Garibaldi: Italo trains—Italy's new, privately run high-speed service to Florence, Rome, and Naples—use Porta Garibaldi Station, north of the city center and not far from Milano Centrale. High-speed TGV trains from Paris also use this station. As Milan's busiest commuter station, Porta Garibaldi is also served by many bus lines and Metro line 2 (green).

By Car: Leonardo never drove in Milan. Smart guy. Driving is bad enough in Milan to make the €20/day fee for a downtown garage a blessing. If you're driving, do Milan (and Lake Como) before or after you rent your car, not while you've got it. If you have

MILAN

a car, use the well-marked suburban *parcheggi* (parking lots), which offer affordable (€6/day) and safe parking at city-edge subway stations, with easy access to the center by Metro.

By Plane: Frequent shuttle trains and buses connect the airports and Milano Centrale train station both conveniently and economically. See "Milan Connections" at the end of this chapter.

Helpful Hints

Theft Alert: Be on guard. Milan's thieves target tourists, especially at the central train station, getting in and out of the subway, and around the Duomo. They can be dressed as tourists, businessmen, or beggars, or they can be gangs of too-young-to-arrest children. Watch out for ragged people carrying newspaper and cardboard—they'll thrust this item at you as a distraction while they pick your pocket. If you're ripped off and plan to file an insurance claim, fill out a report with the police (Police Station, "Questura," Via Fatebenefratelli 11, Metro: Turati, open daily 24 hours, tel. 02-62261). For police emergencies, call 113.

US Consulate: It's at Via Principe Amedeo 2/10 (Metro: Turati, tel. 02-290-351 for recorded info and phone tree, http://milan.usconsulate.gov).

Medical Help: Dial 118 for medical emergencies. There are two medical clinics with emergency care facilities: the **International Health Center** in Galleria Strasburgo (Mon-Thu 9:00-19:00, Fri 9:00-18:00, closed Sat-Sun, between Via Durini and Corso Europa, at #3, third floor, Metro: San Babila, tel. 02-7634-0720), and the **American International Medical Center** at Via Mercalli 11 (Mon-Fri 9:00-17:30, closed Sat-Sun, Metro: Missori or Crocetta, call for appointment, tel. 02-5831-9808, mobile 335-570-1055). A 24-hour pharmacy is in the central train station; look for the neon-green cross.

Street Markets: Milan has two very popular flea markets. **Fiera di Sinigallia** spills into a lot at Porta Genova every Saturday (8:30-17:00, Metro: Porta Genova). If you continue along Viale d'Annunzio to Viale Papiniano, you'll run into the **Papiniano** market (Tue 7:00-13:00 and Sat 7:30-17:00). Small street markets are held every morning except Sunday in various neighborhoods; *Hello Milano* has a complete listing (www.hellomilano.it).

Internet Access: Underground, in the Duomo Metro station, the **Secure Money Center** offers Internet access (€2/30 minutes).

Bookstores: The handiest major bookstore, with fiction and guidebooks in English, is **La Feltrinelli,** under the Galleria Vittorio Emanuele II (daily 10:00-23:00, enter through Autogrill restaurant on Piazza del Duomo, tel. 02-8699-6903).

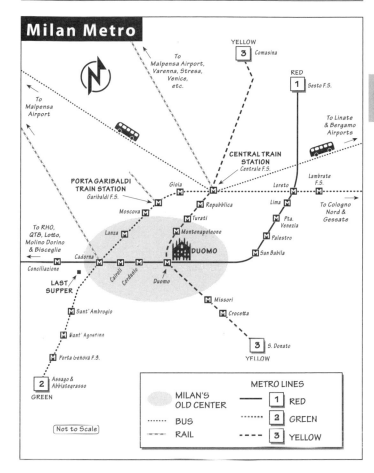

The **American Bookstore** is at Via Camperio 16, near Sforza Castle (Mon-Sat 10:30-19:00, closed Sun, tel. 02-878-920).

Travel Agencies: You can buy train tickets and reserve an overnight berth *(cuccetta)* at the **365 Travel Agency**'s train station locations (listed earlier, under "Arrival in Milan") or at any number of downtown travel agencies.

Getting Around Milan

By Public Transit: Use Milan's great subway system. The clean, spacious, fast, and easy three-line Metro zips you nearly anywhere you may want to go, and trams and city buses fill in the gaps. The handiest Metro line for a quick visit is the yellow line 3, which connects the central train station to the Duomo. The other lines are red (1) and green (2). "ATM" is the acronym for the Milan public transit system. Public transit usually runs until about midnight.

A **ticket,** valid for 75 minutes, can be used for one subway, tram, or bus ride, including a transfer either within the same or another system, but not a round-trip on the same system (€1.50; sold at newsstands, tobacco shops, shops with *ATM* sticker in window, and at machines in subway stations—select the "Urban Tickets" button).

Validate tickets in the machines at the turnstiles, and keep them until you exit the Metro system. If you're caught riding on an unvalidated ticket, you'll be fined €33.

Other ticket options include a *carnet* (€14 for 10 rides—one magnetic ticket that can be validated 10 times); a **24-hour pass** (€4.50, worthwhile if you take at least four rides); and a **48-hour pass** (€8.25). Passes use the same validation machines as standard tickets.

For transit information, visit the **ATM Point** (at Duomo stop, near Arengario exit, to right of Duomo as you face it, opposite La Scala ticket office, Mon-Sat 7:45-19:15, closed Sun, tel. 800-808-181, www.atm-mi.it).

I've keyed sightseeing to the subway system. Though most sights are within a few blocks of each other and the city is perfectly flat, Milan can be an exhausting city for walking. With the Metro, you'll rarely wait more than five minutes for a train. The well-marked trams can also be useful, especially to get to *The Last Supper* (tram #16) and the Monumental Cemetery (#12 or #14).

By Taxi: Small groups go cheap and fast by taxi (drop charge-€3.20, €1.10/kilometer; €5.20 drop charge on Sun and holidays, €6.20 from 21:00 to 6:00 in the morning). It can be easier to walk to a taxi stand than to flag down a cab. Handy stands are at Piazza del Duomo and in front of Sforza Castle (tel. 02-8585 or 02-6969).

By Bike: Locals use bikes to get around quickly and easily. Like many big cities in Europe, Milan has a public bike system, **BikeMi**. You can set up a temporary subscription (€6/week or €2.50/day) online or at an "ATM Point" public transit info office (a handy one is in the Duomo Metro station—see earlier). You'll receive a user code and password, allowing you to pick up a bike at any BikeMi station, generally located near Metro stations. Enter your code and password on the keypad, grab the assigned bike, and you're on your way. The system is designed for short uses (first 30 minutes free, then €0.50/each 30 minutes up to 2 hours, then €2/hour, www.bikemi.com, toll-free tel. 800-808-181).

Tours in Milan

Bus Tours

The three-hour **Autostradale** bus-and-walking tour is a good value, has a live guide describing the city's monuments in English, and guarantees you'll see Leonardo's *Last Supper*—useful if you haven't booked ahead for this important sight. The jam-packed itinerary also includes visits to the Duomo, Galleria Vittorio Emanuele II, Sforza Castle, and La Scala Opera House (€60, departs Tue-Sun at 9:30 and Fri-Sat at 13:00, no Mon tours; off-season no Fri-Sat 13:00 tours). They also offer an express version of the same tour, which skips the walking portion and lasts 1.5 hours (€35, Tue-Sun at 11:00). Tours leave from Piazza del Duomo, next to the taxi stand at the far end of the square from the church. There are four ways to reserve this tour: Book online at least two days in advance at www.autostradale.it; ask your hotelier to book it for you; call the main TI at 02-7740-4343; or drop into the Autostradale office next to the TI at Piazza Castello 1 (Mon-Fri 8:30-18:00, Sat-Sun 9:00-16:00). Tickets may be available for the same-morning departure. To confirm details, call 02-7200-1304 or 02-3391-0794.

Zani Viaggi does a similar tour that includes *The Last Supper*. Guides lead two-language tours (always English, plus one other), departing Tuesday through Sunday at 9:30 and 14:30 from their office at Foro Bonaparte 76, near Sforza Castle (€65, 3.5 hours, no Mon tours; ticket office open Mon-Fri 9:00-19:00, Sat-Sun 9:00-15:00; online reservations must be made at least two days in advance, tel. 02-867-131, www.zaniviaggi.it, excursions @zaniviaggi.it).

CitySightseeing Milano has hop-on, hop-off buses that do a circuit of the major sights accompanied by a recorded commentary. With one ticket, you can get off at a stop, tour the sight, and hop back on the bus to resume your tour. While you can hop on at any of their stops, it's handiest at the Duomo (next to the taxi stand) and La Scala (€20/day—valid until 18:00, €25/48 hours, buy on board; April-Oct daily 9:30-19:25, 2/hour; Nov-March daily 9:30-17:30, hourly; tel. 02-867-131. www.city-sightseeing.it).

Local Guide

Lorenza Scorti is a hardworking young guide who knows her city's history and how to teach it (€135/3-hour tour, €270/day, same price for individuals or groups, evenings OK, mobile 347-735-1346, lo-renza.scorti@libero.it). **Sara Cerri** is another good licensed local guide who enjoys teaching (€175/3 hours, then €50/hour, mobile 380-433-3019, www.walkingtourmilan.it, walkingtourmilan@gmail.com).

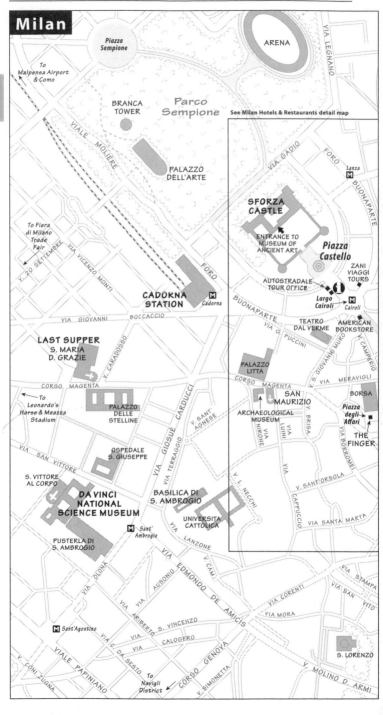

MILAN

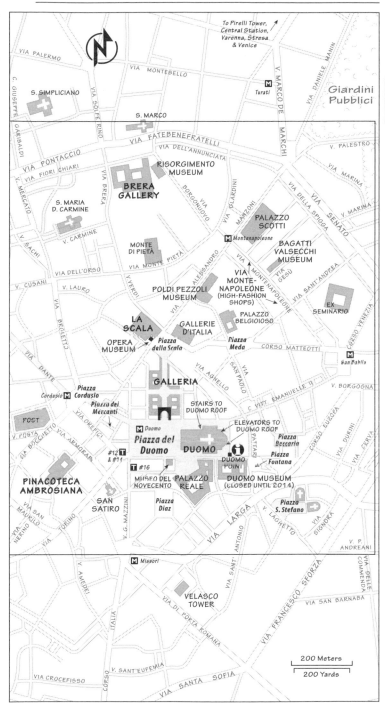

Sights in Milan

▲▲Duomo (Cathedral)

The city's centerpiece is the fourth-largest church in Europe (after the Vatican's, London's, and Seville's). At 525 by 300 feet, the place

is immense, with more than two thousand statues inside (and another thousand outside) and 52 one-hundred-foot-tall, sequoia-size pillars representing the weeks of the year and the liturgical calendar. If you do two laps, you've done your daily walk. It was built to hold 40,000 worshippers, the entire population of Milan when construction began. Ride the elevator or hike to the rooftop for a stroll through its forest of jagged spires.

Cost and Hours: Free entry; separate charges for treasury (€2), baptistery (€4), and roof climb (by **elevator**-€12, daily 9:00-18:00, may close later in high season, enter outside at north or south transept; or take **stairs**-€7, daily 9:00-20:15, until 19:30 in winter, last stair entry at 18:15, enter outside on north side, across from La Rinascente department store). Church open daily 7:00-19:30, Metro: Duomo, tel. 02-7202-2656, www.duomomilano.it.

Crowd-Beating Tips: The **Duomo Point** info center, behind the cathedral on the right-hand side, sells tickets for the Duomo's elevator and stairs. To avoid long ticket lines at the church, buy your ticket here, then go directly through the turnstile (daily 9:00-18:00, tel. 02-7202-3375, staff are helpful and speak English). The outdoor kiosk in front of, but not affiliated with, the info center also sells tickets for the same price during the same hours.

Dress Code: Modest dress is required. Don't wear shorts or anything sleeveless. Even kids with bare shoulders or knees are likely to be turned away at the door.

Audioguide: €5, Mon-Sat 8:30-17:00, no rentals Sun, 1.5 hours, available from kiosk immediately inside church.

Photography: The Duomo charges €2 for a special wristband (sold at audioguide kiosk) that allows you to take pictures.

Background

Back when Europe was fragmented into countless tiny kingdoms and dukedoms, the dukes of Milan wanted to impress their counterparts in Germany and France. Their goal was to earn Milan recognition and respect from both the Vatican and the kings and

princes of northern Europe by building a massive, richly orna-
mented cathedral. Even after Renaissance-style domes were in
vogue elsewhere in Italy, conservative Milan's cathedral stayed on
Gothic target. The dukes—thinking northerners would relate better to Gothic—loaded it with pointed arches and spires. For good
measure, the cathedral was built not from ordinary stone, but from
marble, top to bottom. Pink Candoglia marble was rafted in from
a quarry about 60 miles away, across Lake Maggiore and down a
canal to a port at the cathedral.

Built from 1386 to 1810, with the final touches added in 1965,
this construction project originated the Italian phrase for "never-
ending": "like building a cathedral." It started out Gothic (best
seen in the apse behind the altar) and was finished in the early
1800s under Napoleon (particularly the noteworthy west facade,
which is wonderful late in the day, with the sun low in the sky).
While the church is a good example of the Flamboyant, or "flame-
like," overripe final stage of Gothic, architectural harmony is not
its forte.

Self-Guided Tour of the Duomo

Begin by looping around the Duomo's exterior, then head inside to
enjoy its remarkable bulk, fine stained-glass windows, and Baroque
altar.

Exterior

Walk around the entire church exterior and notice the statues,
made between the 14th and 20th centuries by sculptors from all
over Europe. There are hundreds of these statues—each different and quite creative. Look at the statues on the tips of the many
spires...they seem so relaxed, like they're just hanging out, waiting
for their big day. Functioning as drain spouts, the 96 fanciful gar-
goyle monsters are especially imaginative.

As you stand outside at the back of the church, behind the
altar, imagine the glory of this first wall. These were the earliest
stones, laid in 1390. The sun-in-rose window was the proud symbol
of the city's leading Visconti family; it's flanked by the angel telling
Mary she's going to bear the Messiah. And behind you is a shrine
to the leading religion of the 21st century: soccer. The Football
Team store is filled with colorful vestments and relics of local soccer saints (go upstairs, daily 10:00-19:00).

Continue circling the cathedral. Back at the front, enjoy the
statues enlivening the facade. The lower ones—full of energy and
movement—are early Baroque, from about 1600. Of the five doors,
the center one is biggest. Made in 1907 in the Liberty Style, it features the Joy and Sorrow of the Virgin Mary. Sad scenes are on the
left, joyful ones on the right, and on top is the coronation of Mary

Milan at a Glance

▲▲**Duomo** Milan's showpiece cathedral, with an amazing roof you can walk on, amid a forest of spires. **Hours:** Church—daily 7:00-19:30, rooftop elevator—daily 9:00-18:00, may close later in high season; rooftop stairs—daily 9:00-20:15, until 19:30 in winter, last entry at 18:15. See page 14.

▲▲**Galleria Vittorio Emanuele II** Glass-domed arcade on the main square, perfect for window-shopping and people-watching. **Hours:** Always open. See page 21.

▲▲**La Scala Opera House and Museum** The world's most prestigious opera house. **Hours:** Museum daily 9:00-12:30 & 13:30-17:30. See page 23.

▲▲**Pinacoteca Ambrosiana** Oldest museum in Milan, with works by Raphael, Leonardo, Botticelli, Titian, and Caravaggio, and a special exhibit of Leonardo sketches (until 2015). **Hours:** Tue-Sun 10:00-18:00, closed Mon. See page 25.

▲▲**Basilica di Sant'Ambrogio** Historic, art-packed church dating to early Roman times. **Hours:** Mon-Sat 10:00-12:00 & 14:30-18:00, Sun 15:00-17:00. See page 28.

▲▲*The Last Supper* Leonardo da Vinci's masterpiece, displayed in the Church of Santa Maria delle Grazie, and viewable only with a reservation—book several months in advance. **Hours:** Tue-Sun 8:15-18:45 (last entry), closed Mon. See page 29.

▲**Piazza del Duomo** Milan's main square, full of energy, history, and pickpockets. **Hours:** Always open. See page 20.

▲**Museo del Novecento** Milan's 20th-century art collection, housed in the fascist-era City Hall. **Hours:** Mon 14:30-19:30, Tue-Wed, Fri, and Sun 9:30-19:30, Thu and Sat 9:30-22:30. See page 22.

▲**Gallerie d'Italia** Two adjacent palaces filled with 19th- and 20th-century Italian art. **Hours:** Tue-Sun 9:30-19:30, Thu until 21:30, closed Mon. See page 24.

▲**Church of San Maurizio** The "Sistine Chapel of Lombardy," gorgeously frescoed by Bernardino Luini, a follower of Leonardo. **Hours:** Tue-Sun 9:30-17:30, closed Mon. See page 27.

▲**Leonardo da Vinci National Science and Technology Museum** Leonardo's designs illustrated in wooden models, plus a vast collection of historical, scientific, and technological bric-a-brac and machines. **Hours:** Tue-Fri 9:30-17:00, Sat-Sun 9:30-18:30, closed Mon. See page 29.

▲**Brera Art Gallery** World-class collection of Italian paintings (13th-20th century), including Raphael, Caravaggio, Gentile da Fabriano, Piero della Francesca, Mantegna, and the Bellini brothers. **Hours:** Tue-Sun 8:30-19:00, closed Mon. See page 32.

▲**Risorgimento Museum** History of Italian unification. **Hours:** Tue-Sun 9:00-13:00 & 14:00-17:30, closed Mon. See page 33.

▲**Sforza Castle** Milan's castle containing a museum whose highlight is an unfinished Michelangelo *Pietà*. **Hours:** Tue-Sun 9:00-17:30, closed Mon. See page 34.

▲**Via Dante** Human traffic frolics to lilting accordions on one of Europe's longest pedestrian-only boulevards. **Hours:** Always open. See page 36.

▲**Naviglio Grande** Milan's old canal port—once a working-class zone, now a trendy, atmospheric nightspot for dinner or drinks. **Hours:** Always open. See page 37.

▲**Monumental Cemetery** Evocative outdoor art gallery with tombs showcasing expressive art styles from 1870 to 1930. **Hours:** Tue-Sun 8:00-18:00, closed Mon. See page 38.

Poldi Pezzoli Museum Italian paintings (15th-18th century), weaponry, and decorative arts. **Hours:** Wed-Mon 10:00-18:00, closed Tue. See page 33.

Bagatti Valsecchi Museum 19th-century Italian Renaissance furnishings. **Hours:** Tue-Sun 13:00-17:45, closed Mon. See page 33.

Leonardo's Horse Gargantuan equestrian monument built according to Leonardo's designs. **Hours:** Tue-Sun 9:00-17:30, closed Mon. See page 37.

in heaven by Jesus, with all the saints and angels looking on. Step up close and study the fine reliefs.

Interior

Enter the church. Stand at the back of the fourth-longest nave in Christendom. The apse at the far end was started in 1386. The wall behind you wasn't finished until 1520. Even though the Renaissance had begun, builders stuck with the Gothic style. The two single stone-marble pillars behind you are the most precious ones in the church.

Notice two tiny lights: The little red one on the cross above the altar marks where a nail from the cross of Jesus is kept. This relic was brought to Milan by St. Helen (Emperor Constantine's mother) in the fourth century, when Milan was the capital of the Western Roman Empire. It's on display for three days a year (in mid-Sept). Now look high to the right, in the rear corner of the church, and find a tiny pinhole of white light. This is designed to shine a 10-inch sunbeam at noon onto the bronze line that runs across the floor, indicating where we are on the zodiac (but local guides claim they've never seen it work).

Stained-Glass Windows: Wander deeper into the church, up the right aisle. Check out the windows: 15th-century mosaics of brilliant and expensive colored glass (stained, not painted). Bought by wealthy families seeking the Church's favor, they face the south and get the most light. The altars below generally honor the patron who made each window possible. Pick out familiar scenes in the windows. The purpose was to teach the illiterate masses the way to salvation through stories of the Old Testament and the life of Jesus. On the opposite wall (left side), many of the windows are more modern—from the 16th to the 20th century—and are either made of dimmer, cheaper painted glass or are replacements for ones destroyed by the concussion of WWII bombs that missed the church but fell nearby.

There are a couple of stops of interest along the right aisle. Under the third window, you can trace the uninterrupted rule of 144 local archbishops back to A.D. 51.

The fifth window dates from 1470, just 90 years after the first stone of the cathedral was laid. The window shows the story of Jesus, from Annunciation to Crucifixion. In the bottom window, as the angel Gabriel tells Mary the news, the Holy Spirit (in the form of a dove) enters Mary's window and world. Compare the exquisite beauty of this window to the cruder 19th-century window on the right.

While construction up to this point was very fast, the church wasn't finished for centuries. Below this fifth window, check out the 1888 proposed plan for the west facade. (This plan wasn't used; the west front of the church was finally finished around 1900.)

The seventh window is modern, from the 1980s. Bright and bold, it celebrates two local cardinals (whose tombs and bodies are behind glass). This memorial to Cardinal Ferrari and Cardinal Schuster, who heroically helped the Milanese out of their post-WWII blues, is a reminder that this great church is more than a tourist attraction—it's a living part of Milan.

Altar: Belly up to the bar facing the high altar. While the church is Gothic, the area around the altar is Baroque—a dramatic stage-like setting, in the style of the Vatican in the 1570s (a Roman Catholic statement to counter the Protestant churches of the north, which were mostly Gothic). Napoleon crowned himself King of Italy under this dome in 1805. Now look to the rear up at the ceiling and see the fancy "carving" (between the ribs)—nope, that's painted. It looks expensive, but paint is more affordable than carved stone.

St. Bartolomeo Statue: Find the bald statue lit by the open door, by the wall in the south transept. This is a grotesque 16th-century statue of St. Bartolomeo, an apostle and first-century martyr skinned alive by the Romans. Walk behind the poor guy wearing his own skin like a robe to see his face, hands, and feet. Carved by a student of Leonardo da Vinci, this is a study in human anatomy learned by dissection, forbidden by the Church at the time.

Floor: Walk toward the altar and around the corner 30 steps, to a gate blocking entry to the apse. Look down at the fine 16th-century inlaid-marble floor. The pieces around the altar are original. You can tell that the black marble (quarried from Lake Como) is harder because it looks and feels less worn than the other colors (the white is from Lake Maggiore, the pink from Verona).

Windows: The apse is lit by three huge windows, all 19th-century painted copies. The originals, destroyed in Napoleonic times, were made of precious stained glass.

Other Sights in the Duomo

Crypt of St. Charles Borromeo and Treasury: Steps lead under the altar to the treasury and to the tombs of St. Charles Borromeo (1538-1584, the economic power behind the church) and his family. Charles was bishop of Milan, and the second most important hometown saint after St. Ambrose. Tarnished silver reliefs around the ceiling show scenes from Charles' life. The treasury, or *tesoro*, features empty reliquaries and carved ivories.

Paleo-Christian Baptistery: In the rear of the church (buy ticket at bookshop kiosk, same hours as the Duomo), you can climb down into the church that stood here long before the present one. Milan was an important center of early Christianity. In Roman

MILAN

times, Mediolanum's street level was 10 feet below today's level. You'll see the scant remains of an eight-sided baptistery (where saints Augustine and Ambrose were baptized) and a little church. Back then, since you couldn't enter the church until you were baptized (which didn't happen until age 18), churches had a little "holy zone" just outside for the unbaptized. This included a baptistery like this one.

Cathedral Rooftop: This is the most memorable part of a Duomo visit. You'll wander through a fancy forest of spires with great views of the city, the square, and—on clear days—the crisp and jagged Alps to the north. And, 330 feet above everything, La Madonnina overlooks it all. This 15-foot-tall gilded Virgin Mary is a symbol of the city.

You can climb the stairs or take the elevator; the entrances to both are outside the church (for specifics, see "Cost and Hours," earlier).

Near the Duomo, on or near Piazza del Duomo

▲▲Duomo Museum (Museo del Duomo)

This fine museum, currently closed for extensive renovation, offers an excellent opportunity to understand Milan's cathedral and see its original art close up. It may reopen as early as 2014; inquire locally for details.

▲Piazza del Duomo

Milan's main square is a classic European scene and a popular local gathering point. Professionals scurry, fashion-conscious kids loiter, and young thieves peruse.

Standing in the square (midway between the statue and the Galleria), you're surrounded by history. The **statue** is Victor Emmanuel II, first king of Italy. He's looking at the grand Galleria named for him. The words above the triumphal arch entrance read: "To Victor Emmanuel II, from the people of Milan."

Opposite the Galleria are the twin fascist buildings of the Arengario Palace, which houses the new **Museo del Novecento** (described later). Mussolini made grandiose speeches from their balconies. Study the buildings' relief panels, which tell—with fascist melodrama—the history of Milan. Between these buildings and the cathedral (set back a bit) is the historic ducal palace, **Palazzo Reale.** This building, now a venue for temporary art exhibits, was redone in the Neoclassical style by Empress Maria Theresa in the late 1700s, when Milan was ruled by the Austrian Habsburgs. For a fine view of the Duomo and the piazza, enter the fascist-style building closest to the cathedral through the museum, and go to the bar on the first floor (no ticket necessary, fine *aperitivo* happy hour). Behind the Duomo is a vibrant pedestrian shopping zone along Corso Vittorio Emanuele.

Behind the Victor Emmanuel II statue (opposite the cathedral, about a block beyond the square), hiding in a small courtyard, is **Piazza dei Mercanti,** the center of medieval Milan (described later).

▲▲Galleria Vittorio Emanuele II

A symbol of Milan is its great four-story glass-domed arcade on the cathedral square. This great iron-and-glass structure (part of the age of Eiffel) was symbolic of a new modern era. Built during the heady days of Italian unification (c. 1870), it was the first building in town to have electric lighting, and from its inception, it provided an elegant and popular meeting place. (Sadly, its designer, Giuseppe Mengoni, died the day before the gallery opened.) Here you can turn an expensive cup of coffee into a good value by enjoying some of Europe's best people-watching.

The venerable **Bar Camparino** (at the entry), with a friendly staff and a Liberty-style interior typical of the age, is the former haunt of famous opera composer Giuseppe Verdi and conductor Arturo Toscanini, who used to stop by after their performances at La Scala. It's a fine place to enjoy a drink and people-watch (€3.50 for an espresso is a great deal if you relax and enjoy the view, or €1 at the bar just to enjoy the sumptuous interior). Once called the Campari café (after the wealthy family who originally owned it), this is considered the birthplace of the famous Campari bitter (€4.50 standing or €10 seated, Tue-Sun 7:30-20:00, closed Mon and Aug, tel. 02-8646-4435).

Wander around the gallery. Its art celebrates the establishment of Italy as an independent country. Around the central dome, patriotic mosaics symbolize the four major continents (sorry, Australia). The mosaic floor is also patriotic. The white cross in the center represents the king. The she-wolf with Romulus and Remus (on the south side—facing Rome) honors the city that, since 1870, has been the national capital. On the west side (facing Torino, the provisional capital of Italy from 1861-1865), you'll find that city's symbol: a *torino* (little bull). For good luck, locals step on his irresistible little testicles. Two local girls explained to me that it works better if you spin—two times, and it must be clockwise. Find the poor little bull and observe for a few minutes...it's a cute scene. With so much spinning, the mosaic is replaced every few years.

The gallery has held luxury shops from the beginning. Along with Gucci, Louis Vuitton, and Prada, you'll find Borsalino (at the end near Piazza della Scala), which has been selling hats here since the gallery opened in 1877.

If you cut through the Galleria to the other side, you'll pop out at Piazza della Scala, with its famous opera house and the Gallerie d'Italia (all described later).

▲Museo del Novecento

Milan's 20th-century art fills the twin buildings of Arengario Palace, Mussolini's fascist-era City Hall, facing Piazza del Duomo. In the beautifully laid-out museum, you'll work your way up the escalators and through the last century, one decade at a time. The first painting, at the top of spiral staircase, is *The Fourth Estate* by Pellizza da Volpedo, painted in 1901. It celebrates the socialism and humanitarian spirit that came with the arrival of the new century, preparing you for the spirit of the collection. The first rooms feature the work of Umberto Boccioni, a seminal Futurist working in Milan when the city was at the artistic forefront. His abstract scenes convey the speed and intensity of the new modern age. Along with paintings, there are sculptures from the 1930s by Arturo Martini and Fausto Melotti. Each section is well-described in English, and the capper is a fine panoramic view over Piazza del Duomo through grand fascist-era arches.

Cost and Hours: €5, audioguide-€5, Mon 14:30-19:30, Tue-Wed, Fri, and Sun 9:30-19:30, Thu and Sat 9:30-22:30, last admission one hour before closing, Pallazzo dell'Arengario at Via Marconi 1, tel. 02-8844-4061, www.museodelnovecento.org.

Piazza dei Mercanti

This small square, the center of political power in 13th-century Milan, hides one block off Piazza del Duomo (directly opposite the cathedral). A strangely peaceful place today, it offers a fine smattering of historic architecture that escaped the bombs of World War II.

The arcaded, red-brick building that dominates the square was the City Hall (Palazzo dei Regione). The market was held under the arcades below, with six gates representing the six main guilds. Facing the square (opposite the wellhead), the balcony with the coats of arms is where new laws were announced. Eventually two big families—Visconti and Sforza—took power, Medici-style, in Milan; the snake is their symbol. Running the show in Renaissance times, these dynasties shaped much of the city we see today, including the Duomo and the fortress. In 1454, the Sforza family made peace with Venice while enjoying a friendship with the Medici in Florence (who counseled them on becoming dominant as bankers), and ushered in a time of stability and peace, as the region's major city-states were run by banking families. This freed up money for that Renaissance generation to make art, not war.

This square also held the Palace of Justice (the 16th-century courthouse with the clock tower), the market (not food, but crafts: leather, gold, and iron goods), the bank, the city's first university, and its prison. All the elements of a great city were right here on the "Square of the Merchants."

On Piazza della Scala

To reach these sights, simply cut through the Galleria Vittorio Emanuele II from Piazza del Duomo.

Piazza della Scala

This smart little traffic-free square, out the back between the Galleria and the opera house, is dominated by a statue of Leonardo da Vinci. The statue (from 1870) is a reminder that Leonardo spent his best 20 years in Milan, with well-paid, steady work. He was the brainy darling of the Sforza family (who dominated Milan as the Medici family dominated Florence). Under the great Renaissance genius stand four of his greatest "Leonardeschi." (He apprenticed a sizable group of followers.) The reliefs show his various contributions as painter, architect, and engineer. Leonardo, wearing his hydro-engineer hat, re-engineered Milan's canal system, complete with locks. (Until the 1920s, Milan was one of Italy's major ports, with canals connecting the city to the Po River and Lake Maggiore.)

The statue of Leonardo is looking at a plain but famous Neoclassical building, arguably the world's most prestigious opera house (described next).

▲▲La Scala Opera House and Museum

Milan's famous Teatrale alla Scala opened in 1778 with an opera by Antonio Salieri (of *Amadeus* fame). Today, opera buffs can get a glimpse of the theater and tour the adjacent museum's extensive collection.

Cost and Hours: Museum—€6, daily 9:00-12:30 & 13:30-17:30, last entry 30 minutes before closing, Piazza della Scala, tel. 02-8879-7473, www.teatroallascala.org.

Museum: Well-described in English, the collection features things that mean absolutely nothing to the hip-hop crowd: Verdi's top hat, Rossini's eyeglasses, Toscanini's baton, Fettuccini's pesto, original scores, diorama stage sets, costumes, busts, portraits, and death masks of great composers and musicians. The museum allows you to peek into the actual theater. The stage is as big as the seating area on the ground floor. (You can see the towering stage box from Piazza della Scala across the street.) A recent five-year renovation corrected acoustical problems caused by WWII bombing and subsequent reconstruction. The royal box is just below your vantage point, in the center rear. Notice the massive chandelier made of Bohemian crystal.

Events in the Opera House: The show goes on at the world-famous La Scala Opera House. Schedules vary, but the opera season is nearly year-round (show time 20:00), and ballet and classical concerts are held from October through June. No performances are held in August (for information, call Scala Infotel Service, daily 9:00-18:00, tel. 02-7200-3744; for automated booking, call 02-860-775 and press 2 for English; or book online at www.teatroallascala.org). On the opening night of an opera, a dress code is enforced for men (suit and tie).

Tickets generally go on sale one month before a performance. Seats sell out quickly. On performance days, 140 sky-high gallery tickets are sold at a discount only at the box office (located down the left side of the theater toward the back on Via Filodrammatici, and marked with *Biglietteria Serale* sign). If you want a same-day discounted (but still not cheap) ticket, show up at 13:00 to get your name on the list. Return at 17:00 for the roll call. You must be present when your name is called in order to receive a voucher, which you'll then show at the ticket window to purchase a discounted ticket. One hour before show time, the box office sells any remaining tickets at a 25 percent discount. You can also buy tickets—but not the discounted ones—at a handy ticket office in the Duomo Metro station (daily 12:00-18:00, entrance is to right of the Duomo as you face it, underground, follow signs to *ATM Point*), as well as on the Internet (Web sales end one hour before show time).

▲Gallerie d'Italia

This museum fills two adjacent palaces on Piazza della Scala with the amazing art collections of two banks that once occupied these buildings. One palace dates from the 19th century and boasts the nicest Neoclassical interior I've seen in Milan; the other is 20th-century, Tiffany-like Historicism, with a hint of the coming Liberty Style. Impressive buildings in their own right, they are filled with the exquisite work of 19th- and 20th-century Italian painters. One has Romantic landscapes; Hyperrealistic, time-travel scenes of folk life; and Impressionism. And in the adjacent palace, marble reliefs by Antonio Canova are displayed in appropriately Neoclassical rooms, while upstairs you'll find dramatic scenes from the Risorgimento—showing the thrilling story of the unification of Italy. You can even go downstairs and peer into the original bank vault, which now stores racks and racks of paintings not on display.

Cost and Hours: Free entrance, free audioguides (for as long as the bank is feeling generous), Tue-Sun 9:30-19:30, Thu until 21:30, closed Mon, across from La Scala Opera House at Piazza della Scala 6, toll-free tel. 800-167-619, www.gallerieditalia.com.

West of the Duomo

These are listed roughly in the order you'll reach them, as you travel west from Piazza del Duomo. The first one is just a few short blocks from the cathedral, while the last is just over a mile away.

▲▲Pinacoteca Ambrosiana (with Leonardo exhibit)

This oldest museum in Milan was inaugurated in 1618 to house Cardinal Federico Borromeo's painting collection. And until 2015, the museum is both more expensive and more important, thanks to a long-running special exhibit displaying 22 pages from Leonardo's notebook. Think of your visit in two parts: the permanent collection of paintings (including the Leonardo Hall), and the last room, which has the notebook pages. While it's exciting to see the pages, the permanent material is still the highlight. Pick up the English-language map locating major works, and rent the €1 audioguide (80 minutes), which explains highlights of both the permanent and special exhibits.

Cost and Hours: €15, Tue-Sun 10:00-18:00, closed Mon, last entry at 17:00, near Piazza del Duomo at Piazza Pio XI 2, tel. 02-8069-2221, www.ambrosiana.eu.

Visiting the Museum: Pinacoteca Ambrosiana began as a teaching academy, which explains its many replicas of famous works of art. Highlights include original paintings by Botticelli, Caravaggio, and Titian.

As Cardinal Borromeo was a friend of **Jan Brueghel,** you'll find an entire room (#7) filled with delightful works by Brueghel and other Flemish masters. Study the wonderful detail in Brueghel's *Allegory of Fire* and *Allegory of Water.* The Flemish paintings are extremely detailed—many painted on copper to heighten the effect—and offer an insight into the psyche of the age. If the cardinal were asked why he enjoyed paintings that celebrated the secular life, he'd likely say, "Secular themes are God's book of nature."

Filling an entire wall, **Raphael's cartoon** served as an outline for the famous *School of Athens* fresco at the Vatican Museum. (A cartoon—*cartone* in Italian—is a large charcoal-on-canvas sketch that functions as a model for the making of a fresco.) While the Vatican's much-adored fresco is attributed entirely to Raphael, it was painted mostly by his students. But this *cartone* was wholly sketched by the hand of Raphael. To make the fresco, his assistants riddled this cartoon with pinpricks along the outlines of the characters, stuck it to the wall of the pope's study, and then applied a colored powder. When they removed the *cartone*, the characters' shapes were marked on the wall, and completing the fresco was a lot like filling in a coloring book. If you've seen the original fresco at the Vatican, you'll notice that the figure of Michelangelo (as a brooding stonecutter lounging on the steps in the foreground) is missing from the cartoon. Raphael added him to the fresco as a tribute after seeing Michelangelo's awe-inspiring work on the ceiling of the Sistine Chapel.

As Leonardo da Vinci spent many of his most productive years working in Milan, the city has an affinity for the Renaissance genius. The **Leonardo Hall,** with more of the gallery's permanent collection, features Leonardo's *Portrait of a Musician*, a copy of *The Last Supper*, and several fine Leonardo-type paintings by Bernardino Luini and other disciples. During his Milan years, Leonardo created *The Last Supper* and painted several other famous canvases. Of these other paintings, only the *Portrait of a Musician*—as delicate, mysterious, and thought-provoking as the *Mona Lisa*—remains in Milan. The large fresco filling the far wall—with Christ receiving the crown of thorns—is by Luini. I find the painting of *The Last Supper* most interesting. When the cardinal realized that Leonardo's marvelous frescoed original was fading, he commissioned a careful copy to be created here for posterity. Today, this copy gives a rare chance to appreciate the original colorful richness of the now-faded masterpiece.

The Leonardo Hall leads into the somber library called Federiciana Hall, where you'll find the special **Leonardo exhibit.** The gallery, which owns Leonardo's *Codex Atlanticus,* is showing 22 of its 1,119 pages in themed exhibits changing quarterly until 2015. Soft period music accompanies your time with the 22 glass cases, each displaying a well-lit page from the notebook (the audioguide, which explains each page of the current exhibit, is essential to fully enjoy your visit). Don't enter the special exhibit until you are done with the permanent collection, as it's a one-way system and re-entry isn't allowed.

Piazza degli Affari and a Towering Middle Finger

This square and monument mark the center of Milan's financial district. The bold fascist buildings in the neighborhood were built in the 1930s under Mussolini. Italy's major stock exchange, the Borsa, faces the square. Stand in the center, appreciate the modern take on ancient aesthetics (you're standing atop the city's ancient Roman theater), and find the stern statues representing various labors and occupations, and celebrating the nobility of workers—typical whistle-while-you-work fascist themes. Then notice the equally bold modern statue in the center. After a 2009 contest to find the most appropriate sculpture to grace the financial district, this was the winner. Of course, Italy has its financial problems, and a similar sentiment that powers the Occupy Movement in the US rumbles in this society as well. Here we see how "the 99 percent" feel when they stand before the symbol of corporate power in Italy. (Notice how the finger is oriented—it's the 1 percent, and not the 99 percent, that's flipping the bird.) The 36-foot-tall, Carrara marble digit was made by Maurizio Cattelan, the most famous—or, at least, most controversial—Italian sculptor of our age. *L.O.V.E.,* as the statue is titled, was temporary at first. But locals liked it, and, by popular demand, it's now permanent.

▲Church of San Maurizio

This church, part of a ninth-century convent built into a surviving bit of Milan's ancient Roman wall, dates from around 1500. Despite its simple facade, it's a hit with art lovers for its amazing cycle of Bernardino Luini frescos. Stepping into this church is like stepping into the Sistine Chapel of Lombardy.

Cost and Hours: Free, Tue-Sun 9:30-17:30, closed Mon, Corso Magenta 15 at the Monastero Maggiore, tel. 02-8645-0011.

Visiting the Church: Bernardino Luini (1480-1532), a follower of Leonardo, was also inspired by his contemporaries Michelangelo and Raphael. Sit in a pew and take in the art, which has the movement and force of Michelangelo and the grace and calm beauty of Leonardo.

Maurizio, the patron saint of this church, was a third-century Roman soldier who persecuted Christians, then converted, and eventually worked to stop those same persecutions. He's the guy standing on the pedestal in the upper-right, wearing a bright yellow cape. The nobleman who paid for the art is to the left of the altar. His daughter, who joined the convent here and was treated as a queen (as nuns with noble connections were), is to the right. And all around are martyrs—identified by their palm fronds.

The adjacent **Hall of Nuns,** where sisters were cloistered, is also full of fine paintings. Stepping into this fine room, behind the altar you'll find more amazing art, including fine Luini frescos above and around the wooden crucifix. The Annunciation scene on the arch features a cute Baby Jesus zooming down from heaven. The organ dates from 1554, and the venue, with its fine acoustics, is popular for concerts with period instruments. Explore the pictorial

MILAN

Bible behind the wooden chairs. Luini's landscapes, which line the walls, were groundbreaking in the 16th century. Leonardo incorporated landscapes into his paintings, but Luini was among the first to make landscape the main subject of the painting.

In the adjacent archaeological museum, you can see part of the ancient city wall and a third-century Roman tower.

▲▲Basilica di Sant'Ambrogio

One of Milan's top religious, artistic, and historic sights, this church was first built on top of an early Christian martyr's cemetery by St. Ambrose around A.D. 380, when Milan had become the capital of the fading (and Christian) Western Roman Empire.

Cost and Hours: Free, Mon-Sat 10:00-12:00 & 14:30-18:00, Sun 15:00-17:00, Piazza Sant'Ambrogio 15, tel. 02-8645-0895, www.basilicasantambrogio.it.

❍ Self-Guided Tour: Ambrose was a local bishop and one of the great fathers of the early Church. He helped establish the Church by convincing Augustine, a pagan, to become Christian. (Augustine himself later became another great Church father.) The original fourth-century church was later (in the 12th century) rebuilt in the Romanesque style you see today.

The entry is an arcaded **atrium**—standard in many churches back when you couldn't actually enter the church until you were baptized. The non-baptized waited here during Mass. The courtyard is textbook Romanesque, with playful capitals and fanciful animals. Inset into the wall (right side, above the pagan sarcophagi) are stone markers of Christian tombs—a reminder that this church, like St. Peter's at the Vatican, is built upon an ancient Roman cemetery.

From the atrium, marvel at the elegant 12th-century **facade,** or west portal. It's typical Lombard medieval style. The local bishop would bless crowds from its upper loggia. As two different monastic communities shared the church and were divided in their theology, there were also two different bell towers.

Step into the **nave** and grab a pew. The mosaic in the apse features Jesus Pantocrator (creator of all) in the company of Milanese saints. Around you are pillars with Romanesque capitals and surviving fragments of 12th-century frescos that once covered the church.

The 12th-century **pulpit** sits atop a Christian sarcophagus dating from the year 400. Study its late-Roman and early-Christian iconography—Apollo on his chariot morphs into Jesus on a chariot. You can see the moment when Jesus gave the Old Testament (the first five books, anyway) to his apostles.

The precious, ninth-century golden **altar** has four ancient porphyry columns under an elegant Romanesque 12th-century canopy. The entire ensemble was taken to the Vatican during World

War II to avoid destruction. That was smart—the apse took a direct hit in 1943. The 13th-century mosaic was destroyed; today we see a reconstruction.

Step into the **crypt,** under the altar, to see the skeletal bodies of three people: Ambrose (in the middle, highest) and two earlier Christian martyrs whose tombs he visited before building the church.

Nearby: For a little bonus after visiting the church, consider this: The **Benedictine monastery** next to the church is now Cattolica University. With its stately colonnaded courtyards designed by Renaissance architect Donato Bramante, it's a fine student environment. It's fun to poke around and imagine being a student here.

▲Leonardo da Vinci National Science and Technology Museum (Museo Nazionale della Scienza e Tecnica "Leonardo da Vinci")

The spirit of Leonardo lives here. Most tourists visit for the hall of Leonardo—the core of the museum—with designs illustrated in wooden models. But Leonardo's mind is just as easy to appreciate by paging through a coffee-table edition of his notebooks in any bookstore. The rest of this immense collection of industrial cleverness is fascinating, with planes, trains, automobiles, ships, radios, old musical instruments, computers, batteries, telephones, chunks of the first transatlantic cable, interactive science workshops, and a 1960s "pocket-sized" submarine. Many exhibits include English descriptions. Some of the best exhibits (such as the Marconi radios) branch off the Leonardo hall. Ask for an English museum map from the ticket desk—you'll need it. Allow at least 1.5 hours here. On weekends, this museum is very popular with families, so come early or be prepared to wait in line.

Cost and Hours: €10, guided tour of submarine-€8; Tue-Fri 9:30-17:00, Sat-Sun 9:30-18:30, closed Mon; Via San Vittore 21, bus #50 or #58 from Sforza Castle, or tram #16—catch it just off Piazza del Duomo in direction: San Siro, or Metro: Sant'Ambrogio; tel. 02-485-551, www.museoscienza.org.

▲▲Leonardo da Vinci's *The Last Supper (Cenacolo)*

Housed in the Church of Santa Maria delle Grazie, this is one of the ultimate masterpieces of the Renaissance. Milan's leading family, the Sforzas, hired da Vinci to decorate the dining hall of the Dominican monastery that adjoins the church. This gift was essentially a bribe to the monks so that the Sforzas could locate their family tomb in the church. Ultimately, the French drove the Sforzas out of Milan, they were never buried here, and the Dominicans got a great fresco for nothing. Note that this is a small but very popular sight, and entry must be booked several months in advance (see "Reservations," later).

Cost and Hours: €8, includes €1.50 reservation fee (9:30 and 15:30 visits require €3.25 extra for provided guided English tour). Open Tue-Sun 8:15-18:45 (last entry), closed Mon. Show up 20 minutes before your scheduled entry time. When an attendant calls your time, get up and move into the next room.

Reservations: Reservations are mandatory. Even though the hype surrounding *The Da Vinci Code* novel and movie has died down, spots are still booked several months in advance—so plan ahead. To minimize the humidity problem—even though the damage has already been done—only 900 visitors a day are allowed in. That's 25 tourists popping in every 15 minutes for exactly 15 minutes. Prior to your appointment time, you wait in several rooms to dehumidify, while doors close behind you and open up slowly in front of you. The posted information about Leonardo is mainly in Italian.

If you book by **phone,** you'll have a greater selection of days and time slots to choose from, since the website doesn't reflect cancellations, but you won't be able to reserve same-day tickets (tel. 02-9280-0360, or from the US dial 011-39-02-9280-0360, office open Mon-Sat 8:00-18:30, closed Sun; the number is often busy—once you get through, dial 2 for an English-speaking operator; the process takes about two minutes and you'll hang up with an appointed entry time and a number; pay with credit card upon booking).

If you book **online** using the official website, www.cenacolovinciano.net, choose "Cenacolo Vinciano." You'll see a calendar that shows available time slots for the current month. If the days are blank, it means that all the slots for those days have been filled. Be careful when you select the date—on European calendars, the first day of the week is Monday. If you can't find a spot when you need it, try calling instead, because cancellations show up on the website as booked slots.

Last-Minute Tickets: While "reservations are required," if spots are available (more likely on weekdays and first thing in the morning), you can sometimes book one at the desk (even if the *Sold Out* sign is posted). If fewer than 25 people show up for a particular time slot, you may get lucky. But those who show up without a reservation generally kill lots of time waiting around. Note that the Autostradale and Zani Viaggi bus tours (see "Tours in Milan," earlier) include entry to *The Last Supper*.

Audioguide: Consider the fine €3 audioguide. Its spiel fills every second of the time you're in the room—so try to start listening to it just before you enter (ideally in the waiting room while studying the reproduction of *The Last Supper*).

Photography: No photos are allowed.

Getting There: Take the Metro to Cadorna or Conciliazione (plus a 5-minute walk), or hop on tram #16 (catch it just off Piazza del Duomo on corner of Via Mazzini and Via Dogana), which drops you off in front of the Church of Santa Maria delle Grazie. The Science and Technology Museum (previous listing) is two blocks away.

Visiting *The Last Supper*: Because of Leonardo's experimental fresco technique, deterioration began within six years of *The Last Supper's* completion. The church was bombed in World War II, but—miraculously, it seems—the wall holding *The Last Supper* remained standing. A 21-year restoration project (completed in 1999) peeled away 500 years of touch-ups, leaving Leonardo's masterpiece faint but vibrant.

In a big, vacant whitewashed room, you'll see faded pastels and not a crisp edge. The feet under the table look like negatives. But the composition is dreamy—Leonardo captures the psychological drama as the Lord says, "One of you will betray me," and the apostles huddle in stressed-out groups of three, wondering, "Lord, is it I?" Some are scandalized. Others want more information. Simon (on the far right) gestures as if to ask a question that has no answer. In this agitated atmosphere, only Judas (fourth from left and the only one with his face in shadow)—clutching his 30 pieces of silver and looking pretty guilty—is not shocked.

The circle meant life and harmony to Leonardo. Deep into a study of how life emanates in circles—like ripples on a pool hit by a pebble—Leonardo positioned the 13 characters in a semicircle. Jesus is in the center, from whence the spiritual force of God emanates, or ripples out.

The room depicted in the painting seems like an architectural extension of the church. The disciples form an apse, with Jesus as the altar—in keeping with the Eucharist. Jesus anticipates his sacrifice, his face sad, all-knowing, and accepting. His feet even foreshadowed his death by crucifixion. Had the door, which was cut out in 1652, not been added, you'd see how Leonardo placed Jesus' feet atop each other, ready for the nail.

The room was a refectory or dining room for the Dominican friars. Traditionally, they'd gather here to eat, with a Last Supper scene on one wall facing a Crucifixion scene on the opposite wall.

The perspective is mathematically correct. In fact, restorers found a tiny nail hole in Jesus' left eye, which anchored the strings Leonardo used to establish these lines. The table is cheated out to show the meal. Notice the exquisite lighting. The walls are lined with tapestries (as they would have been), and the one on the right is brighter in order to fit the actual lighting in the refectory (which has windows on the left). With the extremely natural effect of the light and the drama of the faces, Leonardo created a masterpiece.

North of the Duomo, in the Brera Neighborhood

▲Brera Art Gallery

Milan's top collection of Italian paintings (13th-20th century) is world-class, but it can't top Rome's or Florence's. Established in 1809 to house Napoleon's looted art, it fills the first floor above a prestigious art college.

Cost and Hours: €6, more during special exhibits, Tue-Sun 8:30-19:00, closed Mon, last entry 45 minutes before closing, free lockers just before the ticket counter, no photos, Via Brera 28, Metro: Lanza or Montenapoleone, tel. 02-722-631, www.brera. beniculturali.it. Since there are no English descriptions, consider renting the audioguide (€5, ID required).

Visiting the Museum: Enter the grand courtyard of a former monastery, where you'll be greeted by the nude *Napoleon with Tinkerbell* (by Antonio Canova). Climb the stairway (following signs to *Pinacoteca*, past all the art students), buy your ticket, and pick up an English map of the museum's masterpieces.

The gallery's highlights include works by late-Gothic master Gentile da Fabriano, hinting at the realism of the coming Renaissance (check out the lifelike flowers and realistic, bright gold paint—he used real gold powder, Room IV). Andrea Mantegna's *The Dead Christ* is a textbook example of feet-first foreshortening (Room VI). Room XVIII hosts a permanent glass-enclosed restoration lab, allowing you to see various restoration works in progress.

In Room XXI, notice how Crivelli employs Renaissance technique (he was a contemporary of Leonardo), yet clings to the mystique of the Gothic Age (that's why I like him so much). Find eight Crivellis. Also, don't miss Raphael's *Wedding of the Madonna*, Piero della Francesca's *Madonna and Child with Four Angels* (Room XXIV), and the gritty-yet-intimate realism of Caravaggio's *Supper at Emmaus* (Room XXIX). Room XXXV features several of Canaletto's picture-postcards of Venetian cityscapes. This is ahead-of-its-time Impressionism—there's not a single line in these works, just strategically placed daubs of paint that render palazzos and canals bathed in Venetian light with photographic precision. To spice things up, look for Francesco Hayez's hot and heavy *The Kiss (Il Bacio)* in Room XXXVII. You'll also find paintings by the great Venetian masters Tintoretto and Veronese.

MILAN

Java junkies will seek out the great, cheap cappuccino machine: Go through Napoleon's courtyard and straight through the art school to the end of the long hall; the machine's on your left. It's fun to explore the art school on the ground floor, mill about among the many young students, and wonder if there's a 21st-century Leonardo in your midst.

▲Risorgimento Museum

With a quick 30-minute swing through this quiet one-floor museum, you'll get an idea of the interesting story of Italy's rocky road to unity: from Napoleon (1796) to the victory in Rome (1870). However, there isn't much information in English. It's just around the block from the Brera Art Gallery at Via Borgonuovo 23.

Cost and Hours: €2, Tue-Sun 9:00-13:00 & 14:00-17:30, closed Mon, Metro: Montenapoleone, tel. 02-8846-4176, www.museodelrisorgimento.mi.it.

Northeast of the Duomo, near Montenapoleone

Poldi Pezzoli Museum

This classy house of art features top Italian paintings of the 15th through 18th century, old weaponry, and lots of interesting decorative arts, such as a roomful of old sundials and compasses.

Cost and Hours: €9, Wed-Mon 10:00-18:00, closed Tue, last entry one hour before closing, free English audioguides, Via Manzoni 12, Metro: Montenapoleone, tel. 02-794-889, www.museopoldipezzoli.it.

Bagatti Valsecchi Museum

This unique 19th-century collection of Italian Renaissance furnishings was assembled by two aristocratic brothers who spent a wad turning their home into a Renaissance mansion. The beautiful but outrageously expensive café in its Renaissance courtyard might be worth the €5 cover charge just to be seen sipping tea with Milan's stylish elite.

Cost and Hours: €8, half-price on Wed, open Tue-Sun 13:00-17:45, closed Mon, free English audioguides and good English descriptions throughout, Via Gesù 5, Metro: Montenapoleone, tel. 02-7600-6132, www.museobagattivalsecchi.org.

Sforza Castle and Nearby
▲Sforza Castle (Castello Sforzesco)

The castle of Milan tells the story of the city in brick. Built in the late 1300s as a military fortress, it guarded the gate to the city wall and defended Milan from enemies "within and without." It was beefed up by the Sforza duke in 1450 in anticipation of a Venetian attack. Later, the Sforza family made it their residence and built their Renaissance palace into the fortress. It was even home to their in-house genius, Leonardo. (When he applied for a position with the Sforza family, he did so as a military engineer and contributed to the design of the ramparts.) During the time of foreign rule (16th-19th century), it was a barracks for occupying Spanish, French, and Austrian soldiers. And today it houses an array of museums. While your ticket covers all the museums (including Egyptian, music, and furniture), the Museum of Ancient Art is the one to visit.

Cost and Hours: €3, free entry 16:30-17:00 and Fri 14:00-17:00; open Tue-Sun 9:00-17:30, closed Mon, WCs and free lockers at the ticket counter, English info fliers throughout and at information office beside the Porta Umberto entrance, Metro: Cairoli, tel. 02-8846-3700, www.milanocastello.it.

➲ Self-Guided Tour: This tour begins outside the fortress, then focuses on the Museum of Ancient Art.

The **gate** facing the city center stands above a ditch that was once filled with water. A relief celebrates Umberto I, the second king of Italy. Above that, a statue of St. Ambrose, the patron of Milan (and a local bishop in the fourth century), oversees the action. Notice the chart, just outside the gate, showing how the city was encircled first by a crude medieval wall, and then by a state-of-the-art 16th-century wall—of which this castle was a key element. It's apparent from the enormity of these walls that Milan was a strategic prize. Today, the walls are gone, giving the city two circular boulevards.

This immense brick fortress—exhausting at first sight—can only be described as heavy. While originally functioning as military parade grounds, today its three huge courtyards host concerts and welcome the public. (The holes in the walls were for scaffolding.)

Just past the ticket counter, the **Museum of Ancient Art** fills the old Sforza family palace with interesting medieval armor, furniture, early Lombard art, and—for your finale—Michelangelo's unfinished *Pietà Rondanini*. While the museum is huge, here are room-by-room highlights leading you to Michelangelo's *Pietà*.

In the first room, among ancient sarcophagi (with early Christian themes), stands a fine 14th-century **equestrian statue**—a memorial to Bernabò Visconti. Of the four virtues, he selected only two (strength and justice) to stand beside his anatomically correct horse, opting out of love and patience.

Next, the room of **tapestries** is dominated by a big embroidery of St. Ambrose defeating the heretical Arians. While that was a fourth-century struggle, 12 centuries later, he was summoned back in spirit to deal with Protestants, in the form of Archbishop Borromeo. As a Counter-Reformation leader, with St. Peter's Basilica behind him, Ambrose stands tall and strong in defense of the Roman Church. The room is lined by 16th-century Flemish tapestries, which were easy to pack up quickly as the nobility traveled. These were typical of those used to warm chilly stone palaces.

Next, you'll come to the **Sala delle Asse,** named for the mulberry garden that was used to feed silkworms. The Visconti family grew rich making silk in the Lake Como area. While plastered over for centuries, this room was restored around 1900. Not much sparkle survives, but you can appreciate the intricate canopy woven with branches and rope in complicated knots—the work of Leonardo himself, in 1498. The tiny Leonardo-esque painting of Madonna and Child is by Francesco Napoletano, a pupil of Leonardo. The painting's structure, anatomy, and subtle modeling of the color with no harsh lines *(sfumato)* are all characteristic of Leonardo. In the upper right, notice the castle, as it looked in 1495.

After browsing a room filled with weapons and armor from the 16th and 17th centuries, you reach the highlight of the museum—**Michelangelo's *Pietà Rondanini.*** This

is a rare opportunity to enjoy a Michelangelo statue with no crowds. Michelangelo died while still working on this piece, his fourth *pietà*. A *pietà*, by definition, is a representation of a dead Christ with a sorrowful Virgin Mary. While unfinished and seemingly a mishmash of corrections and reworks, it's a thought provoking work by a genius at nearly 90 years old, who knows he's fast approaching the end of his life. The symbolism is of life and of death: Jesus returning to his mother, as two bodies seem to become one.

Michelangelo's more famous *pietà* at the Vatican (carved when he was in his 20s) features a beautiful, young, and astonished Mary. Here, Mary is older and wiser. Perhaps Mary is now better able to accept death as part of life...as is Michelangelo. The *pietà* at the Vatican is simple and clear, showing two different people: the mother holding her dead son. Contemplating the *Pietà Rondanini,* you wonder who's supporting whom. It's confused and complex, each figure seeming to both need and support the other.

This unfinished statue is unique in that it shows the genius of Michelangelo midway through a major rework—Christ's head is cut out of Mary's right shoulder, and an earlier arm is still just hanging there. Above Mary's right ear, you can see the remains of a previous face (eye, brow, and hairline).

And there's a certain power to this rawness. Walk around the back to see the strain in Mary's back (and Michelangelo's rough chisel work) as she struggles to support her son. The sculpture's elongated form hints at the Mannerist style that would follow.

Notice the ancient Roman altar underneath the *Pietà*. Notice, also, the funeral portrait of Michelangelo, showing the artist as he looked when he died in 1564, working on this statue—still vibrant and seeking.

For a quick exit, continue past the *Pietà* exit, out the back side and into Sempione Park (described next).

Parco Sempione

This is Milan's equivalent of Central Park. With its circa 1900 English-style gardens, free Liberty-style aquarium, views of the triumphal arch, and sprawling family-friendly grounds, this park is particularly popular on weekends.

A five-minute walk through the park, on the left, is the erector-set **Branca Tower** (Torre Branca). You'll ride an elevator that takes you as high as the Mary that crowns the cathedral, for a commanding city view (€4, hours are erratic—call or confirm at TI before heading out, closed Mon and in bad weather, tel. 02-331-4120).

At the far end of the park is the monumental **Arco della Pace**. Originally an arch of triumph, it comes with Nike, goddess of victory, commanding a six-horse chariot. It was built facing Paris to welcome Napoleon's rule and to celebrate the ideals of the French Revolution, destined to lift Italy into the modern age. When they learned Napoleon was just another megalomaniac, they turned the horses around, their tails facing France. With Italian unification in the 1860s, its name was changed to "Arch of Peace."

▲Via Dante

This grand pedestrian boulevard and popular shopping street leads from Sforza Castle toward the town center and the Duomo. Via Dante was carved out of a medieval tangle of streets to celebrate Italian unification (c. 1870) and make Milan—the home of the king—a worthy capital city. Consequently, all the facades lining it are relatively new. Over the vigorous complaints of merchants, the street became traffic-free in 1995. Today, they'd have it no other way, and the street is popular with local shoppers and office workers on lunch breaks. Enjoy strolling this beautiful people zone, where you'll hear the whir of bikes and the lilting melodies of accordion players instead of traffic noise. Photo exhibits are frequently displayed up and down the street. In front of Sforza Castle, a commanding statue of Giuseppe Garibaldi, one of the heroes of the unification movement, looks down one of Europe's longest pedestrian zones. From here you can walk to the Duomo and beyond (about 1.5 miles), down streets that are all nearly traffic-free. Stroll and appreciate Italian design both in people and in windows (ignore the Foot Locker).

Away from the Center

▲Naviglio Grande (Canal District)

Milan, although far from any major lake or river, has a sizable port. It's called "The Big Canal." Since 1170, a canal has connected Milan with the Mediterranean via the Ticino River (which flows into the Po River on its way to the Adriatic Sea). Five hundred years ago, Leonardo helped further develop the city's canals and designed a modern lock system. Then, during the booming Industrial Age in the 19th century—and especially with the flurry of construction after Italian unification—the canals were busy shipping in the marble and stone needed to make Milan the great city it is today. In fact, a canal (filled in in the 1930s) once circled the walls of the city, allowing barges to dock with their stone right at the building site of the great cathedral. By the 1950s, landlocked Milan was actually the seventh-biggest port in Italy, as its canals were instrumental in the rebuilding of the bombed-out city. Today, disused train tracks parallel the canal, old warehouse buildings recall the area's working-class heritage, and former workers' tenements—once squalid and undesirable—are much in demand and being renovated smartly. While recently rough and characteristic, today the area is trendy, traffic-free, pricey, and thriving with inviting bars and eateries. The canal district, with its lively restaurants and bars lining the old industrial canal that once so busily served the city, is an understandably popular destination for dinner or evening fun (for recommendations, see "Eating in Milan," later).

Getting There: Ride the Metro to Porta Genova, exit following signs to Via Casale, and walk the length of Via Casale one block

directly to the canal. To the left, on both sides of the canal, are plenty of great places to eat and drink.

Leonardo's Horse

The largest equestrian monument in the world is a modern reconstruction of a model created in 1482 by Leonardo da Vinci for the Sforza family. The clay prototype was destroyed in 1499 by invading French forces, who used it for target practice. In 1982,

American Renaissance-art collector Charles Dent decided to build the 15-ton, 24-foot-long statue from Leonardo's design, planning to present it to the Italians in appreciation for their role in the Renaissance and in homage to Leonardo's genius. Unfortunately, Dent died before the project could be completed. In 1997, American sculptor Nina Akamu created a new clay model that became the template for the final statue; it was unveiled in 1999. The exhibit, described in English, includes statue casts and photos of the construction.

Cost and Hours: Free, Tue-Sun 9:00-17:30, closed Mon, located on outskirts between San Siro racetrack and Meazza soccer stadium; from the corner of Via Mazzini and Via Dogana, take tram #16, direction: San Siro, to Stratico Palatino stop—ask conductor when to get off, then head right on Via Palatino, and left on Piazzale dello Sport to #9; or you can walk a half-mile from Metro: Lotto.

Soccer

The Milanesi claim that their soccer (football, or *calcio*, in Italian) teams are the best in Europe. For a dose of Europe's soccer mania (which many believe provides a necessary testosterone vent to keep Europe out of a third big war), catch a match while you're here. A.C. Milan and Inter Milan are the ferociously competitive home teams (tickets-€10-350).

A.C. Milan tickets are sold at Intesa Sanpaolo banks (one's at Via Verdi 8, Mon-Fri 8:45-13:45 & 14:45-15:45, closed Sat-Sun), online at www.acmilan.com, or at the Milan Point Shop (Tue-Sat 10:00-19:00, closed Sun-Mon, Piazza XXVI Maggio next to Via San Gottardo). Inter Milan tickets are sold at Banca Popolare di Milano banks (one's at Piazza Meda 4, Metro: San Babila; Mon-Fri 8:45-13:45 & 14:45-15:45, closed Sat-Sun) or online at www.inter.it.

Games are held in the 85,000-seat Meazza stadium most Sunday afternoons from September to June (Metro: Lotto, or tram #16—catch it just off Piazza del Duomo, on corner of Via Mazzini and Via Dogana, direction: San Siro; take it to last stop, where you'll find the stadium). You'll need to have your passport when you buy your ticket and bring it with you to the stadium for security reasons.

▲Monumental Cemetery (Il Cimitero Monumentale)

Europe's most artistic and dreamy cemetery experience, this grand place was built just after unification to provide a suitable final resting spot for the city's "famous and well-deserving men." Any cemetery can be evocative, but this one—with its super-emotional portrayals of the deceased and their heavenly escorts (in art styles c. 1870-1930)—is in a class by itself. It's a vast garden art gallery of proud busts and grim reapers, heartbroken angels and weeping widows, too-young soldiers and countless old smiles, frozen on yellowed black-and-white photos.

MILAN

Cost and Hours: Free, Tue-Sun 8:00-18:00, closed Mon, last entry at 17:30, pick up map at the entrance gate, a long walk from Metro: Garibaldi FS, or catch tram #12 or #14 (stop: Bramante) from the corner of Via Orefici and Via Cantu' near the Duomo, tel. 02-8846-5600, www.monumentale.net.

Shopping in Milan

High Fashion in the Quadrilateral

For world-class window-shopping, visit the "Quadrilateral," an elegant high-fashion shopping area around Via Montenapoleone, northeast of La Scala. This was the original Beverly Hills of Milan. In the 1920s, the top fashion shops moved in, and today it remains *the* place for designer labels. Most shops close Sunday and for much of August. On Mondays, stores open only after 16:00. In this land where fur is still prized, the people-watching is as entertaining as the window-shopping. Notice also the exclusive penthouse apartments with roof gardens high above the scene. Via Montenapoleone and the pedestrianized Via della Spiga are the best streets.

Whether you're gawking or shopping, here's the best route: From La Scala, walk up Via Manzoni to the Metro stop at Montenapoleone, browse down Via Montenapoleone, and cut left on Via Santo Spirito (lined with grand aristocratic palazzos—peek into the courtyard at #7). Then, opposite #17, step into the elegant courtyard at #10 to check out the café-sitters and their poodles. Turn right to window-shop down Via della Spiga, turn right on Via Sant'Andrea and then left, back onto Montenapoleone, which leads you through a final gauntlet of temptations to Corso Giacomo Matteotti, near the Piazza San Babila. Then (for less-expensive shopping thrills), walk back to the Duomo down the pedestrian-only Corso Vittorio Emanuele. From the Duomo, go down Via Dante to Sforza Castle.

Near the Duomo

For a (slightly) more reasonably priced shopping excursion, next to the Duomo, step into **La Rinascente**—a Nordstrom-type department store with something for everyone and an especially good toy selection. Each floor has a fine collection of designer names sold out of independent shops, all functioning within the walls of this vast and venerable store. Simply riding the escalator up and up gives a fun overview of Italian design and marketing. The seventh floor is a top-end food circus, with terrace views of the Duomo and a public WC. Its name, meaning "the place reborn," fits its history. In an earlier life, it was a fine Liberty-style building until it burned down in 1918. It was rebuilt, only to be bombed in World War II and rebuilt once again (Mon-Thu 9:30-21:00, Fri-Sat 9:30-22:00, Sun 10:00-21:00, has a VAT refund office and recommended restaurants, faces north side of the Duomo on Piazza del Duomo).

Heading away from the Duomo, stroll between the arcades on the Corso Vittorio Emanuele II and feel yourself surrounded by tempting material pleasures. Clothing stores that range from classy and pricey to trendy and inexpensive are sheltered under the arcades.

At Via Passarella, detour to the right to check out **Excelsior,** a bold high-end concept store. A conveyor belt takes you from level to colorful level with pulsing music and electronic art installations. If you're looking for the perfect €1,000 shirt, you've come to the right place. Otherwise, hit **Eat's Food Market** in the basement and pick up a tasty high-design salad—a bargain at €6 (daily 10:00-20:30, Galleria del Corso 4, two long blocks behind the Duomo, tel. 027-630-7301).

Double back to the Corso Vittorio Emanuele II to continue shopping all the way to the San Babila Metro station, or return to the Duomo.

Nightlife in Milan

For evening action, check out the artsy Brera area in the old center, with several swanky sidewalk cafés to choose from and lots of bars that stay open late. Home to Brera's Art University, this district has a sophisticated, lively people-watching scene. Another great neighborhood for nightlife, especially for a younger scene, is Naviglio Grande (canal district), Milan's formerly bohemian, now gentrified "Little Venice" (described earlier; Metro: Porta Genova).

There are always concerts and live music playing in the city at various clubs and concert halls. Specifics change quickly, so it's best to rely on the entertainment information in periodicals from the TI.

Sleeping in Milan

All recommended hotels are within a few minutes' walk of Milan's subway system. With Milan's fine Metro, you can get anywhere in town in a flash.

Any time in March, April, September, and October, the city can be completely jammed by conventions, and hotel prices jump way up. I've listed high-season prices, but not convention-gouging prices. (For the convention schedule, see www.fieramilano.it.) Summer is usually wide-open, and prices are discounted, though many hotels close in August for vacation. Hotels cater more to business travelers than to tourists, so Fridays and Saturdays are generally cheaper and available.

Lately I've noticed a trend in which small family-style hotels in the center are being neglected, and the big, modern business-class hotels around the train station are proliferating. I've tried to collect central places, where travelers feel appreciated and the staff feels like part of the family. If the following places are booked up, go online—there are lots of hotels near the train station.

Near the Duomo

The Duomo area is thick with people-watching, reasonably priced eateries, and the major sightseeing attractions. From Milano Centrale train station to the Duomo, it's just four stops on a direct Metro line (yellow line 3, direction: San Donato) to Metro: Duomo.

$$$ Hotel Grand Duca di York is stuck oddly in the middle of banks and big-city starkness three blocks southwest of Piazza del Duomo. It's got lavish public spaces and 33 modern, bright rooms that are thoughtfully designed and decorated (Sb-€98-128, Db-€170-190, 5 percent Rick Steves discount through 2014 if you book direct, air-con, elevator, free Wi-Fi, free minibar, near Metro stops: Cordusio or Duomo, Via Moneta 1, tel. 02-874-863, www.ducadiyork.com, info@ducadiyork.com).

$$$ Hotel Spadari boasts a modern, Art Deco-inspired interior designed by the Milanese artist Giò Pomodoro ("Joe Tomato" in English). The 40 rooms have billowing drapes, big paintings, and designer doors. It's next door to the recommended Peck Deli, and two blocks from the Duomo (standard Db-€230-260, deluxe Db-€290-360, no need for the pricier suites, 5 percent Rick Steves discount through 2014 when you book direct, air-con, elevator, free Wi-Fi, free minibar, Via Spadari 11, tel. 02-7200-2371, www.spadarihotel.com, reservation@spadarihotel.com).

$ Hotel Vecchia Milano is a humble, clean place buried deep in the old town on a narrow lane. Although the management is indifferent, it rents 27 comfortable rooms at a great price for the location (Sb-€65-80, Db-€90-100, air-con, free Wi-Fi, next to recommended Hostaria Borromei at Via Borromei 4, tel. 02-875-042, www.hotelvecchiamilan.com, hotelvecchiamilano@tiscalinet.it).

Between La Scala and Sforza Castle

$$$ Hotel Star, comfortable and modern, rents 30 sparkling, fresh, and spacious rooms with unexpected artistic touches (Sb-€165, Db-€225, prices drop about €40 outside convention times,

MILAN

Sleep Code

(€1 = about $1.30, country code: 39)
S = Single, **D** = Double/Twin, **T** = Triple, **Q** = Quad, **b** = bathroom, **s** = shower only. Unless otherwise noted, credit cards are accepted, English is spoken, and breakfast is included. Many cities in Italy levy a hotel tax of about €2 per person, per night, which must be paid in cash (not included in the rates I've quoted).

To help you sort easily through these listings, I've divided the accommodations into three categories based on the price for a standard double room with bath:

$$$ **Higher Priced**—Most rooms €150 or more.
$$ **Moderately Priced**—Most rooms between €110-150.
$ **Lower Priced**—Most rooms €110 or less.

Prices can change without notice; verify the hotel's current rates online or by email. For the best prices, always book direct.

check website for deals, interior rooms are quieter, air-con, free Wi-Fi, usually closed Aug, Via dei Bossi 5, tel. 02-801-501, www.hotelstar.it, info@hotelstar.it, cheeky Vittoria).

$$$ Antica Locanda dei Mercanti offers 15 white, minimalist rooms in an 18th-century palazzo. While the rooms are all different—some with kitchens, others with spacious terraces—all have a clean, fresh-flower vibe, uncommonly romantic for Milan. (Db-€195-265, €30 more for terrace rooms, air-con, free guest computer and Wi-Fi, Via San Tomaso 6, Metro: Cairoli or Cordusio; tel. 02-805-4080, www.locanda.it, locanda@locanda.it, Alex and Eri).

$$ London Hotel, a simple 30-room hotel with a comfy living-room-like lobby and basic rooms, is tucked away on a quiet side street just off vibrant Via Dante. It's warmly run by the friendly Gambino family: mom and pop Elda and Franco don't speak English, but daughters Tanya and Licia do (S-€80-90, Sb-€90-100, D-€110-140, Db-€130-160, Tb-€170-200, prices much higher during conventions, skip their €8 breakfast and grab something on Via Dante, cheaper in July and Aug, book direct for these rates and get an additional 10 percent off with cash, air-con, elevator, pay Wi-Fi, near Metro: Cairoli at Via Rovello 3, tel. 02-7202-0166, www.hotellondonmilano.com, info@hotellondonmilano.com).

Near Centrale Train Station

The train station neighborhood is more practical than characteristic. Its hotels are utilitarian business-class hotels with prices that bounce all over depending upon the convention schedule. You'll find more shady characters than shady trees in the parks, and lots of massage parlors. But you can't beat the convenience (near station, Metro to the center, shuttles to airports), and if you hit it outside of convention times, the prices are hard to beat. Here are two decent options:

$$ Hotel Florida is a comfortable, well-maintained business-class hotel with 55 rooms on a quiet street one block from the station. Prices plummet if you book direct and are not visiting during a convention (rack rate Db-€290 but often more like Sb-€70-100 and Db-€90-130, free Wi-Fi, Via Lepetit 33, tel. 02-670-5921, www.hotelfloridamilan.com, info@hotelfloridamilan.com). With the tracks to your back, leave the station's upper hall to the left, cross the taxi stand, and then cross the road. The hotel is on Via Lepetit, around the corner from Ristorante Giglio Rosso.

$$ Hotel Garda has 55 tidy, spotless rooms two and a half blocks from the station (Sb-€40-140, Db-€60-170; email first to get a promo code for a 10 percent discount when booking on their website; air-con, elevator, Via N. Torriani 21, tel. 02-6698-2626, www.hotelgardamilan.com, info@hotelgardamilan.com). Exit the train station and head straight across the square, veering left onto Via N. Torriani. It's ahead on your right.

Hostels

For beds costing about €21-30, consider Milan's hostels. Most are away from the center, but the first one I've listed is closer to town.

$ Ostello Burigozzo, a good choice, has 83 beds in both private rooms and in shared dorm rooms (€22-27 for beds in 6-, 8-, 16-, and 24-bed dorms; hotel-type rooms on the third floor—Sb-€50-70, Db-€70-100, Tb-€90-123; reserve ahead, 14:30-24:00 check-in but can leave bags earlier, curfew at 1:30 in the morning, elevator, free guest computer and Wi-Fi, self-serve laundry, Via Burigozzo 11, Metro: Missori—on yellow line 3, tel. 02-5831-4675, www.ostelloburigozzo11.com, info@ostelloburigozzo11.com).

$ AIG Piero Rotta is larger and offers cheap, basic accommodations with a simple breakfast and self-service laundry (€21-30 beds in 2-6-bed dorms, €23-28 for 2-, 3-, and 4-bed rooms with private bath, €2 extra for nonmembers, near Metro: QT8—on red line 1, at Via Martino Bassi 2, tel. 02-3926-7095, www.hostelmilan.org, milano@aighostels.it).

Eating in Milan

Milan's bars, delis, *rosticcerie,* and self-service cafeterias cater to people with plenty of taste and more money than time. You'll find delightful eateries all over town (note that they take Aug off).

I find the price difference between basic and classy restaurants

MILAN

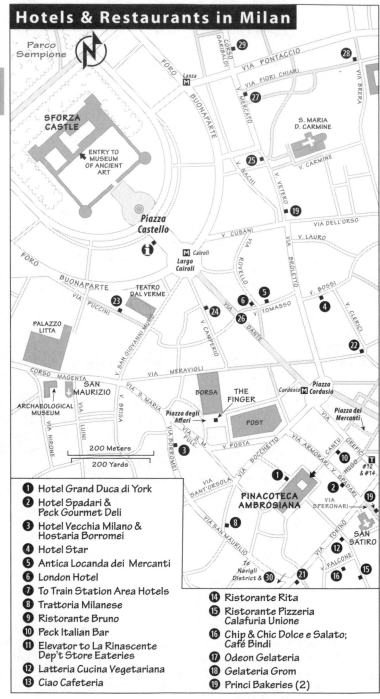

Hotels & Restaurants in Milan

1 Hotel Grand Duca di York
2 Hotel Spadari & Peck Gourmet Deli
3 Hotel Vecchia Milano & Hostaria Borromei
4 Hotel Star
5 Antica Locanda dei Mercanti
6 London Hotel
7 To Train Station Area Hotels
8 Trattoria Milanese
9 Ristorante Bruno
10 Peck Italian Bar
11 Elevator to La Rinascente Dep't Store Eateries
12 Latteria Cucina Vegetariana
13 Ciao Cafeteria
14 Ristorante Rita
15 Ristorante Pizzeria Calafuria Unione
16 Chip & Chic Dolce e Salato; Café Bindi
17 Odeon Gelateria
18 Gelateria Grom
19 Princi Bakeries (2)

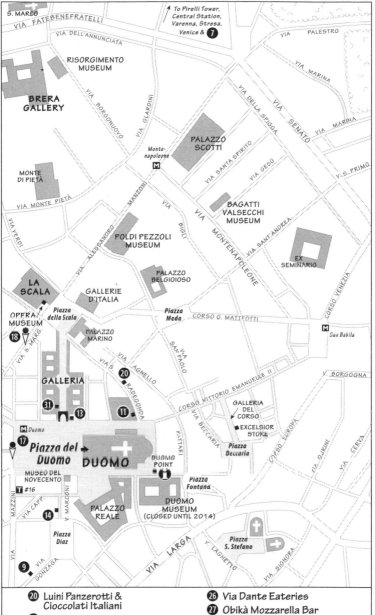

20 Luini Panzerotti &
Cioccolati Italiani

21 Supermarket

22 Victoria Ristorante

23 Da Rita e Antonio

24 Antica Osteria Milanese

25 Convivium Ristorante
and Pizza

26 Via Dante Eateries

27 Obikà Mozzarella Bar

28 Bar Brera

29 Bottega Caffè Cacao

30 To Naviglio Grande Eateries

31 Bar Camparino

to be negligible, so it's worth springing for the places that offer the best experience. To eat mediocre food on a famous street with great people-watching, choose an eatery on the pedestrian-only Via Dante. To eat with students in trendy little trattorias, explore the Brera neighborhood. To eat well near the Duomo, consider the recommended places listed later.

Locals like to precede a lunch or dinner with an *aperitivo* (while Campari made its debut in Milan, a simple glass of *vino bianco* or prosecco, the Italian champagne, is just as popular). Bars fill their counters with inviting baskets of munchies, which are served free with these drinks, at about 17:00. If you're either likable or discreet, a cheap drink can become a light meal.

Milan's signature dishes (often served together as a *piatto unico,* or "single dish") are *risotto alla milanese* and *ossobuco.* The risotto is flavored with saffron, which gives it its intense yellow color. The subtle flavor of the saffron pairs nicely with the *ossobuco* (meaning "marrow," or, literally "hole in the bone," of the veal shank). The prized marrow is extracted with special little forks and is considered the best part of the meal.

Near the Duomo

Dining with Class

Trattoria Milanese, sophisticated and family-run, is a splurge. It has an enthusiastic and local clientele—the restaurant didn't even bother to get a phone until 1988. Expect a Milanese ambience and quality traditional cuisine (Mon-Fri 12:00-14:45 & 19:00-22:45, closed Sat-Sun and mid-July-Aug, evening reservations recommended, air-con, Via Santa Marta 11, 5-minute walk from the Duomo, near Pinacoteca Ambrosiana, tel. 02-8645-1991).

Ristorante Bruno serves Tuscan cuisine with a passion for fresh fish. This place impresses with its dressy waiters, hearty food, inexpensive desserts, and a fine self-serve antipasto buffet (a plate full of Tuscan specialties for €10). You can eat inside or on the sidewalk under fascist columns (Sun-Fri 12:00-15:00 & 19:00-23:00, closed Sat and Aug, moderate prices, air-con, Via M. Gonzaga 6, reservations wise, tel. 02-804-364, Graziella).

Hostaria Borromei is where Milanese yuppies go for power lunches to impress clients with market-fresh traditional Italian dishes. Dine under an awning of vines in an elegant mellow-yellow interior courtyard or in their cantina-chic dining rooms. Reservations are recommended (€12 pastas, €20 *secondi,* Mon-Fri 12:30-14:45 & 19:30-22:45, Sat-Sun 19:30-22:45, Via Borromei 4, tel. 02-8645-3760).

Peck Italian Bar is a hit with the sophisticated office crowd, which mobs the place at lunch for its fast, excellent meals with im-peck-able service. It's owned by the same people who run the recommended high-end Peck Gourmet Deli (listed later), so be prepared to spend—this place's classiness alone makes it worth the money. Any time you find yourself among such a quality-conscious group of Milanesi, you know you're getting good food (€14 pastas, €18 *secondi*, Mon-Fri 7:30-23:00, Sat 9:00-23:00, closed Sun, Via Cantù 3, tel. 02-869-3017).

Dining at the Top of a Top-End Department Store with a Duomo View

The seventh floor of the La Rinascente department store, alongside the Duomo, has a Milanese-style food court. Of its many eateries, three enjoy a sunny outdoor terrace. You'll dine accompanied by views of the cathedral's rooftop (though anyone can pop up for a look at the cathedral). All three of the terrace-seating establishments recommended below are open 9:00-24:00, and can be accessed after store hours from elevators on Via S. Radegonda: **Obikà** is a swanky mozzarella bar offering this heavenly cheese in all its various forms—cow's milk, buffalo, and smoked—in salads or on splittable €12-20 antipasto sampler plates, accompanied by *salumi*, tapenades, and vegetables. Study their English menu to choose cheeses and accompaniments. (Another Obikà is north of the Duomo—see "In the Brera Neighborhood," later.) **Ristorante Maio** has pricey full-meal service (€13 pastas and pizzas, €25 *secondi*). And **Il Bar**, living-room cozy with cushy divans and low coffee tables, serves light meals (salads, pasta), coffee, desserts, and cocktails.

Eating Simply

Latteria Cucina Vegetariana, with a 50-year history, is a bright hole-in-the-wall that serves a good vegetarian Italian lunch. This busy joint—with tight seating in front and behind the kitchen—is overrun with tables where neighborhood workers enjoy soup, salads, pastas, and imaginative veggie entrées at affordable prices. Try the €13 *piatto misto al forno* for a delicious assortment of soufflés, quiches, and roasted and sautéed veggies (€6-12 *panini* and salads, €13-15 meals, Mon-Sat 12:00-16:00, closed Sun, just off Via Torino at Via dell'Unione 6, 2 blocks southwest of the Duomo, tel. 02-874-401).

Ciao, a self-service cafeteria, offers a low-stress, affordable meal above a fast-food arcade on Piazza del Duomo (daily 11:30-23:00, sometimes closes at 22:30, inexpensive pasta and good salad bar, easy public WC). It's to the right of the Galleria entrance—enter through the ground floor Autogrill and go up to the second floor.

Ristorante Rita is a smart budget option (€5 pastas and *secondi*) without the Italian fast-food feel. While the downstairs has

MILAN

a take-out place, there's a sleek, modern restaurant upstairs with good food and cafeteria prices. Their happy hour is a bargain, with a buffet of savory snacks (Mon-Sat 12:00-15:00 & 17:00-20:00, closed Sun, on Via Marconi between Piazza del Duomo and Piazza Diaz, tel. 02-8699-7387).

Ristorante Pizzeria Calafuria Unione is a thriving Milanese-style eatery popular with locals and tourists alike for its pizza and local dishes (€9 pizzas and pastas, €16-20 *secondi*, closed Sun, Metro: Missori, a few blocks south of Piazza del Duomo at Via dell'Unione 8, tel. 02-866-103).

Chip & Chic Dolce e Salato's name says it all: cheap and chic with sweets and salads. This fun little place is a hit with local office workers for its €6 salads in edible bowls, pastas, and fresh pastries (Mon-Sat 12:00-15:00, closed Sun, a couple of blocks south of Piazza del Duomo at Galleria Unione 7, Metro: Missori, mobile 347-035-4761). The **Café Bindi**, across the gallery, has a similar style and charm.

Gelato: Floodlit Mary gazes down on the **Odeon Gelateria** from the top of the Duomo for good reason (next to McDonald's, on far side of square opposite Duomo facade, open nightly until 24:00, closes earlier off-season). While Odeon is convenient, **Gelateria Grom,** two blocks toward La Scala, is the connoisseurs' choice (daily 11:30-23:30, Via Santa Margherita 16).

Picnics Milan-Style, Near the Duomo

Princi bakery is mobbed with locals vying for focaccia, olive breadsticks, and luscious pastries. Notice the stacked-wood-oven action in the back. For most pastry items (like the brioche), pay the cashier first; for items sold by weight (such as pizza and cake), get it weighed before you pay. Consider a pasta lunch (12:00-15:00 only) for €6 per plate (open Mon-Sat 7:00-20:00, Sun 10:00-19:30, on Via Speronari, off Via Torino, a block southwest of Piazza del Duomo; a larger Princi bakery, more like a café, is near Sforza Castle and is listed later).

Peck Gourmet Deli is an aristocratic deli with a fancy café/lunchroom/pastry and gelato shop upstairs, a gourmet grocery and *rosticceria* on the main level, and an expensive *enoteca* wine cellar in the basement. Even if all you can afford is the aroma, peek in. Check out the classic circa-1930 salami slicers and the gourmet assembly line in the kitchen in the back. The *rosticceria* serves fancy food to go for a superb picnic dinner in your hotel. It's delectable, beautiful, sold by weight (order by the *etto*—100-gram unit, 250 grams equals about a half-pound), and pricey (Mon 15:30-19:30, Tue-Sat 9:15-19:30, closed Sun, Via Spadari 9, tel. 02-802-3161).

Luini Panzerotti serves up piping-hot mini-calzones *(panzerotti)* stuffed with mozzarella, tomatoes, ham, or whatever you like for €3-5 (Mon 10:00-15:00, Tue-Sat 10:00-20:00, closed Sun and Aug, Via S. Radegonda 16, tel. 02-8646-1917). From the back of the Duomo, head north and look for the lines of hungry locals out front. Order from the small menus posted behind the cash registers. Traditionally, Milanesi munch their hot little meals on nearby Piazza San Fedele. Don't overlook the *dolce* half of their menu— Panzerotti is popular for its sweets all day long. Across the street is another local hit, **Cioccolati Italiani,** for chocoholics in search of a sweet treat.

Billa Superfresco Supermarket is within a few blocks of the Duomo (Mon-Sat 8:00-23:00, Sun 9:00-21:00, small deli on ground level, big supermarket in basement, on Via Torino at intersection with San Maurilio).

Near La Scala Opera House

Victoria Ristorante is casually elegant, with a modern yet nostalgic atmosphere. It offers creative reinterpretations of traditional Italian dishes for loyal locals and visitors in the know. Its thoughtfully presented dishes, while pricey, are a good value (Mon-Fri 12:30-14:30 & 19:30-24:00, Sat 19:30-24:00, closed Sun, Metro: Cordusio or Duomo, Via Clerici 1, tel. 02-869-0834).

Near Sforza Castle

Da Rita e Antonio is a favorite neighborhood restaurant, serving up well-prepared, reasonably priced Milanese specialties such as *costoletta* (breaded veal chop) and *ossobuco* (veal shank and risotto), as well as delicious €9 Neapolitan-style pizzas. It's a high-energy, brightly lit, dressy place, complete with waiters in bow ties and vests (€10 pastas, €20 *secondi*, great tiramisu, Tue-Sun 12:00-14:30 & 19:00-23:30, closed Mon, Via G. Puccini 2a, tel. 02-875-579). Facing Sforza Castle from the end of Via Dante, it's about 100 yards to your left, built into the far side of the pink-and-white theater.

Antica Osteria Milanese is a hardworking family place with a smart local following and spacious, stylish seating. They serve good-quality typical Milanese favorites (€9 pastas, €14 *secondi*, Mon-Sat 12:15-14:30 & 19:30-22:15, closed Sun, Via Camperio 12, tel. 02-861-367, Alessandro).

Convivium Ristorante and Pizza is popular for its extensive wine list, clever dishes, and conviviality. Classy yet understated, this is a good place for a foodie splurge (€10 pizza and pastas, €22 *secondi*, daily 12:00-14:30 & 19:00-24:00, facing Santa Maria del Carmine church at Via Ponte Vetero 21, tel. 02-8646-3708, Claudio and Nicola).

Princi bakery, near the castle, works the same as the one on Via Speronari (listed earlier), only it's more of a restaurant, with seating both inside and on the street. While the bakery and café are open all day, they serve hot cafeteria-style lunches only 12:00-15:30 (Mon-Sat 7:00-20:00, Sun 9:00-19:30, Via Ponte Vetero 10, tel. 02-7201-6067).

Fancy Via Dante Bars and Cafés: Thriving and central, Via Dante is lined with hardworking eateries where you can join locals for a lively lunch. Or, for about the price of your forgettable hotel breakfast, you can start your day watching the parade of Milanesi heading to work.

In the Brera Neighborhood

The Brera neighborhood, surrounding the Church of St. Carmine, is laced with narrow, inviting pedestrian streets. Make an evening of your visit by having an *aperitivo* (pre-dinner drink) with snacks at recommended Bar Brera or any other bar—most serve munchies with pre-dinner drinks 17:00-21:00. Afterward, stroll along restaurant row on Via Fiori Chiari and Via Brera, or duck into the semicircular lane of Via Madonnina to survey the sidewalk cafés as you pass fortune-tellers, artists, and knock-off handbag vendors.

Obikà is a trendy mozzarella eatery with a sleek, minimalist, jazzy ambience (daily 12:00-15:30 & 18:30-24:00, on corner of Via Mercato and Via Fiori Chiari, Via Mercato 28, tel. 02-8645-0568).

Bar Brera, kitty-corner from the Brera Art Gallery, serves salads, sandwiches, and pastas to throngs of art students. Come during the first hour of happy hour (daily 18:00-21:00), have a seat, order an €8 drink, and then help yourself to the buffet (17:00-19:00), which has a generous variety of *antipasti,* from marinated veggies to prosciutto (buffet is free if you buy drinks; €6 salads, €8-10 plates, great streetside seating, Via Brera 23, tel. 02-877-091).

Bottega Caffè Cacao is a quick and handy place for a light meal. In a casually artisan, modern-rustic setting, savor delightful sandwiches (mini and standard size), colorful salads on crispy flatbread, and an array of coffees. Lines can stretch out the door, but the service is quick. Order at the register, then eat at the counter, upstairs, or on the terrace (€1.50 mini-sandwiches, €3 brioche sandwiches, €5 *panini*, €7 salads, daily 7:30-19:30, Corso Garibaldi 16, one block north of Via Tivoli, tel. 02-8050-6589).

In Naviglio Grande (Canal District)

Consider ending your day at the port of Milan. The Naviglio Grande has a bustling collection of bars and restaurants where you have your choice of memorable and affordable options that come with a great people scene.

Getting There: Ride the Metro to Porta Genova and walk down Via Casale, which dead-ends a block away at the canal. Walk halfway across the metal bridge and survey the scene. The street you just walked has plenty of cheap options, including La Vineria, described next. Most of the action—and all of my other recommendations—are to the left, on or near the canal. Consider doing a reconnaissance stroll before settling in somewhere: Walk down the canal on one side to the bridge with cars, then go back on the other side.

La Vineria is a fun place with streetside seating, serving cheap and fun plates of cheese and meats and wine from giant vats to a cool crowd (daily, June-Sept dinner only from 15:30, Oct-May lunch and dinner except no lunch on Mon, Via Casale 4, tel. 02-8324-2440).

Pizzeria Tradizionale is a local favorite for pizza (daily, at the far end of canal walk, Ripa di Porta Ticinese 7).

Ristorante Brellin is the top romantic splurge, with a dressy crowd and fine food. The menu is international while clinging to a bit of tradition (€14 pastas, €24 *secondi,* daily 12:30-15:30 & 19:00-24:00, behind the old laundry tubs at Vicolo dei Lavandai, tel. 02-5810-1351, www.brellin.it).

Osteria Cucina Fusetti is a charming little place serving good Sardinian cuisine. What's that? Giuseppe speaks English, and he enjoys explaining (€8 pastas, €15 *secondi,* closed Sun; near the curved bridge with the zigzag design at the Japanese restaurant, go away from canal to Via Fusetti 1; mobile 340-861-2676).

Pizzeria Spaghetteria La Magolfa is a local fixture offering good, cheap €5 salads, pastas, and pizzas. You can sit inside, on a veranda, or at a table on the street. For €15, two people could split a hearty pizza and a good bottle of wine and get full...and a bit drunk (no cover, a long block off canal at end of Via M. Fusetti at Via Magolfa 15, tel. 02-832-1696).

Milan Connections

By Train

From Milano Centrale by Train to: Venice (at least hourly, most departures at :05 or :35 past the hour, most are direct on high-speed ES trains, 2.5-3.5 hours), **Florence** (hourly, 1.75 hours), **Genoa** (about hourly, 1.5-2 hours, also look for trains to La Spezia or Livorno that stop at Genoa), **Rome** (hourly, 3-8 hours, overnight possible), **Brindisi** (4 direct/day, 2 are night trains, 9-15 hours, more with changes), **Cinque Terre/La Spezia** (about hourly, 3 hours direct or with change in Genoa; trains from La Spezia to the villages go nearly hourly), **Cinque Terre/Monterosso al Mare** (8/day direct, otherwise hourly, 3-4 hours, more with change in

Genoa), **Varenna** on Lake Como (1 hour; €6.40; small line direct to Lecco/Sondrio/Tirano leaves at 6:20, 7:20, 8:20, 9:20, 10:20, 12:20, 14:20, 16:20, 17:20, 19:20, 20:20, and 21:20; confirm these times—if you take a train at a time not listed here, it will require a change in Lecco and an extra 30 minutes), **Stresa** on Lake Maggiore (about hourly—there can be gaps in service; 1-hour fast train may require reservations; also 1.5-hour slow train; also look for trains to Domodossola and some international destinations that stop at Stresa), **Como** (at least hourly, 30-90 minutes, boats go from Como to Varenna until about 19:00), **Naples** (direct trains hourly, 5 hours, more with change in Rome, overnight possible); see www.trenitalia.com for details.

From Milano Porta Garibaldi by High-Speed Train: While the Centrale Station departures listed above are operated by Trenitalia, a competing private rail company called Italo offers additional high-speed connections to **Florence** (8/day, 2 hours), **Rome** (8/day, 3.5 hours), and **Naples** (5/day, 4.75 hours). While Italo is often cheaper (particularly if you book long in advance), it uses the less convenient Porta Garibaldi Station in Milan, and it doesn't accept railpasses (for details on Italo, visit www.italotreno.it).

International Destinations: Amsterdam (hourly with several changes, fastest via Basel or Zurich, 15 hours), **Barcelona** (14-20 hours, several with 1-5 changes), **Bern** (change required in Brig, at least 3.5 hours), **Frankfurt** (change in Basel or Zurich, at least 9-10 hours), **London** (3/day, 12-18 hours with changes), **Munich** (7/day, 8-12 hours with changes), **Nice** (5/day with change in Ventimiglia, night train possible, 5-6.5 hours), **Paris** (2-3/day direct from Milano Porta Garibaldi, 7 hours; night train possible from Milano Centrale), **Lyon** (8/day, 6-8.5 hours with changes), **Vienna** (1/day direct, more with 1-3 changes, 11-14 hours). With dozens of budget airlines serving Europe's hub cities, flying to your international destination is often the most efficient and economical option.

By Plane

To get flight information for Malpensa or Linate airports or the current phone number of your airline, call 02-74851 or 02-232-323 and wait for English options, or check www.sea-aeroportimilano.it.

Malpensa Airport

Most international flights land at the manageable Malpensa Airport (airport code: MXP), 28 miles northwest of Milan. Customs guards fan you through, and even the security dog seems friendly. You'll most likely land at Terminal 1 (international flights), rather than Terminal 2 (low-cost EU flights); buses connect the two. Both have ATMs (at Terminal 1, between exit 4 and 5 at Banca Na-

MILAN

Train Connections from Milan

zionale del Lavoro), banks, and exchange offices. Terminal 1 has a pharmacy, eateries, and a hotel reservation service disguised as a TI (daily 7:00-20:00; when you exit the baggage-carousel area, go right to reach services and exit; tel. 02-5858-0080).

You have three easy ways to get to downtown Milan: by train, shuttle bus, or taxi.

By Train: The Malpensa Express has two different lines serving downtown Milan. One line serves Milan's central train station, Milano Centrale (€10, 1-2/hour, 40-50 minutes, usually runs until 22:30). The other line zips between the airport and Milan's Cadorna station, which is both a Metro stop and a small train station; it's relatively close to the Duomo and Sforza Castle (€11, €15 same-day round-trip, credit cards accepted, not covered by railpasses, 2/hour, 30 minutes; usually departs airport at :26 and :56 past the hour, generally departs Cadorna at :28 and :58 past the hour, very long hours, tel. 800-500-005, www.malpensaexpress.it).

At the airport, as you pop out through customs, you'll see a *Treno per Malpensa* kiosk selling tickets and a big electric board on the wall indicating how many minutes until the next departure. Follow signs (*Treni* and *Malpensa Express*) down the stairs to the tracks. Check to make sure your train is going to the right destination—*Milano Centrale* or *Milano Cadorna*. When you get off the train, turn to "Arrival in Milan," earlier.

If you're leaving Milan to go *to* the airport, either go to Milan's Centrale Station (check the big departure board for the track number) or take the Metro to the Cadorna stop, surface, and buy a ticket (€11) at the Malpensa Express office in the station. Purchase your ticket before you board. Trains depart Cadorna from track 1; note that there are a few late-night departures to and from Cadorna by bus after midnight—ask when you buy your ticket.

Malpensa Airport also has direct, high-speed rail links to **Florence** (2/day, 2.75 hours), **Rome** (1/day, 4.5 hours), and **Naples** (1/day, 6 hours). Check www.trenitalia.com for details.

By Shuttle Bus: Two bus companies offer virtually identical, competing services between Malpensa Airport and Milan's central train station. They each charge about €10 for the one-hour trip (buy ticket from driver) and depart from the same places: in front of the airport (outside exit 4) and from Piazza Luigi di Savoia (on the east side of Milan's central train station—with your back to the tracks, exit to the left). Buses leave about every 20 minutes, every day, from very early until just after midnight (Malpensa Shuttle tel. 02-5858-3185, www.malpensashuttle.it; Autostradale tel. 02-3391-0794, www.autostradale.it). They're almost comically competitive, with one offering three rides for the price of two. Play around a bit and you may save some money.

By Taxi: Taxis into Milan cost a fixed rate of €90; avoid hustlers in airport halls (catch taxis outside exit 6). Considering how far the city is from the airport and how good the train and bus services are, Milan is the last place I'd take an airport taxi.

Getting Between Malpensa and Linate: The Malpensa Shuttle company runs a bus between the airports about hourly (€13, from Malpensa to Linate runs 7:50-24:25, 1.25 hours, catch bus outside Malpensa's exit 3, stop 20, buy tickets from Airport 2000 offices; from Linate to Malpensa buses depart 4:30-21:30, bus stops at Malpensa's Terminal 1—you must request stop if you need Terminal 2; tel. 02-5858-3185, www.malpensashuttle.it).

Linate Airport

Most European flights land at Linate (airport code: LIN), five miles east of Milan. The airport has a bank with an ATM (just past customs) and a hotel-finding service disguised as a TI (daily 7:30-23:30, tel. 02-7020-0443). You can get to downtown Milan by bus or taxi (or to Malpensa Airport by bus; see above).

By Bus: Two different buses—Starfly and ATM—take you from Linate Airport to downtown. The Starfly bus zips you to the central train station (€5, buy ticket from driver, 3/hour, 30 minutes, bus runs from airport 6:00-22:00, from station 6:00-21:30, leaves from east side of train station at Piazza Luigi di Savoia, tel. 02-587-237, www.autostradale.it). The cheaper ATM city bus gets you to the San Babila Metro stop (specifically to Corso Europa, just around the corner from Piazza San Babila and its Metro station; from here it's one stop to the Duomo on red line 1, direction: Molino Dorino or Bisceglie, or a 7-minute walk). The bus costs €1, departs every 10 minutes, and takes 20 minutes (departures leave city center 5:35-24:35, from airport 6:00-01:05, www.atm-mi.it). Either bus company works fine: Wait for the one that's handier to your hotel, or hop on the first one that shows up. From where it drops you off, take the Metro or a taxi to your hotel. Both buses leave the airport from outside the arrivals hall.

By Taxi: Taxis from Linate to the Duomo cost about €25.

Bergamo (Orio Al Serio) Airport

Some budget airlines, such as Ryanair and Wizzair, use Bergamo Airport—about 30 miles from Milan—as their Milan hub (airport code: BGY, tel. 035-326-323, www.sacbo.it).

An express bus, Orioshuttle, connects the airport to Milan's central train station (€10, daily 4:00-23:15, 2/hour, 1 hour, buy tickets from driver or online at http://ticketonline.orioshuttle.com, tel. 035-330-706). A different company, Oriobus Express, covers the same route (€10, €15 round-trip, daily 4:30-1:00 in the morning, 2/hour, 1 hour, tel. 02-3391-0794, www.autostradale.it).

THE LAKES

Commune with nature where Italy is joined to the Alps, in the lovely Italian lakes district. In this land of lakes, the million-euro question is: Which one? For the best mix of accessibility, scenery, and offbeatness, the village of Varenna on Lake Como is my top choice, followed by Stresa on Lake Maggiore. In either place, you'll get a complete dose of Italian-lakes wonder and aristocratic-old-days romance. Bustling Milan, just an hour away from either lake, doesn't even exist. Now it's your turn to be *chiuso per restauro* (closed for restoration). If relaxation's not on your agenda, the lakes shouldn't be either. If you must choose between Lake Como and Lake Maggiore, the former is a better place to linger, while the latter makes a good day trip from Milan.

Lake Como

Lake Como (Lago di Como)—lined with elegant 19th-century villas, crowned by snowcapped mountains, and busy with ferries, hydrofoils, and slow, passenger-only boats—is a good place to take a break from the intensity and obligatory-turnstile culture of central Italy. It seems like half the travelers you'll meet have tossed their itineraries into the lake and are actually relaxing.

Lake Como is Milan's quick getaway, and the sleepy mid-lake village of Varenna is the gateway to the lake and the handiest base of operations. With good connections to Milan, Malpensa Airport, and mid-lake destinations, Varenna is my favorite home base for the lakes. Today, the hazy, lazy lake's only serious industry is tour-

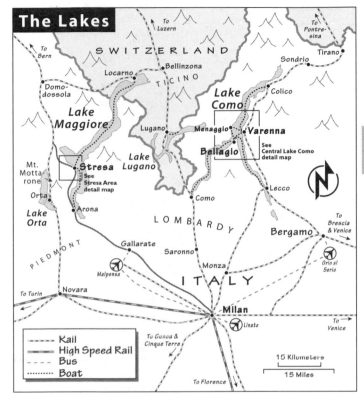

The Lakes

[Map showing: Switzerland, Ticino, Lake Maggiore, Lake Como, Lake Lugano, Lake Orta, Lombardy, Piedmont, Italy. Cities include To Luzern, To Pontresina, Tirano, Sondrio, To Bern, Locarno, Bellinzona, Colico, Domodossola, Lake Como, Menaggio, Varenna, Lugano, Bellagio, Mt. Mottarone, Stresa, Orta, Lecco, Arona, Como, To Brescia & Venice, Bergamo, Gallarate, Saronno, Malpensa, Monza, Orio al Serio, To Turin, Novara, Milan, Linate, To Venice, To Genoa & Cinque Terre, To Florence]

See Central Lake Como detail map

See Stresa Area detail map

LAKES

Rail
High Speed Rail
Bus
Boat

15 Kilometers
15 Miles

ism. Thousands of lakeside residents travel daily to nearby Lugano, in Switzerland, to find work. The lake's isolation and flat economy have left it pretty much the way the 19th-century Romantic poets described it: heaven on earth.

Planning Your Time

Even though there are no essential activities, plan for at least two nights so you'll have an uninterrupted day to see how slow you can get your pulse.

Getting Around Lake Como

By Boat: Lake Como is well-served by boats and hydrofoils. The lake service is divided into three parts: south-north from Como to Colico; mid-lake between Varenna, Bellagio, Menaggio, and Cadenabbia (Villa Carlotta); and the southwestern arm to Lenno (Villa del Balbianello). Unless

Boat Schedule Literacy Tips

Feriali	Monday-Saturday
Festivi	Sundays and holidays
Partenze da...	Departing from
Traghetto or *autotraghetto*	Car ferry (walk-on passengers, too)
Aliscafo or *servizio rapido*	Hydrofoil
Battello ship	Slow passenger-only boat going to Como
Battello navetta	Shuttle serving mid-lake only

you're going through Como, you'll probably limit your cruising to the mid-lake service (boat info: toll-free tel. 800-551-801 or tel. 031-579-211, www.navigazionelaghi.it). Boats go about every 30 minutes between Varenna, Menaggio, and Bellagio (€4.60 per hop, 15-20 minutes, daily approximately 7:00-22:30, confirm return trip when you disembark). The one-day €15 mid-lake pass saves you a little over the cost of four rides. It can be used to make unlimited trips between seven different villages bordering the lake, either on the *autotraghetto* (car ferry) or the passenger-only *battello* (but note that many travelers take only two rides in a day—a round-trip between Varenna and Bellagio). Overnight stopovers aren't allowed, so buy individual tickets for each ride if you aren't planning to return the same day.

The free schedule (available at travel agencies, hotels, and boat docks) lists boat times. Rates are displayed on posters at ticket windows. Confusingly, the schedule requires you to scan four different timetables to know all the departures:

- car and passenger ferry (mid-lake ferryboat, or *autotraghetto*)
- hydrofoil (*servizio rapido*, costs a third more, enclosed, stuffy, speedy, less scenic)
- all-lake slow boat *(battello ship)*
- mid-lake shuttle ferry *(battello navetta)*

If you find the schedule impossible to decipher, simply ask at each dock when the next boat is leaving and which slip it's leaving from (Bellagio has several docks). When checking schedules, be sure to pay attention to whether you're traveling on a weekday (*feriali*, Mon-Sat) or a Sunday or holiday *(festivi)*. Review your possible connections (ask your hotelier for help) before you set out so you can pace your day smartly. It'd be a shame to miss a boat and lose out on a hike or an eagerly anticipated meal because of confusing timetables.

By Car: With scarce parking, traffic jams, and expensive car ferries, this is no place to drive if you don't have to. While you can drive around the lake, the road is narrow, congested, and lined with privacy-seeking walls, hedges, and tall fences. Parking in Bellagio is more difficult than in Varenna. If you have a car in Varenna, leave it there and use the boat.

While you can rent cars in Bellagio, for most travelers, it's best to take the train to Milan and pick up a car there, either at the central train station or at one of Milan's three airports.

Varenna

This community of 800 people offers the best of all lake worlds. Easily accessible by train, on the less-driven side of the lake, Va-

renna has a romantic promenade, a tiny harbor, narrow lanes, and its own villa. It's just the right place to savor a lakeside cappuccino or *aperitivo*. There's wonderfully little to do here, and it's very quiet at night... unless you're here during one of the hundred or so annual American wedding parties. The *passerella* (lakeside promenade, lit at foot level and safe after dark) is adorned with caryatid lovers pressing silently against each other in the shadows. Varenna is a popular destination with my readers and European vacationers—book well in advance for visits in summer (May-Oct). Between November and mid-March, Varenna practically shuts down; hotels close for the winter, and restaurants and shops reduce their hours.

Orientation to Varenna

Tourist Information

The TI (called Proloco Varenna Information Point), on the **main square,** is generally open only during high season (May-Sept Tue-Sat 10:00-12:00 & 15:00-18:00, Sun 9:00-12:00, closed Mon and Oct-April, just past the bank, tel. 0341-830-367, www.discoverva-renna.com). The travel agency, a block from the train station, is a good backup if the TI is closed. Your hotel may have the latest edition of the *Varenna Tourist Info* booklet, with updated info on sights around Varenna and a list of restaurants, services, and day trips.

Arrival in Varenna

By Train: From any destination covered in this book, you'll get to Lake Como via Milan. The quickest, easiest, and cheapest Milan connection to any point mid-lake (Varenna, Bellagio, or Menag-

LAKES

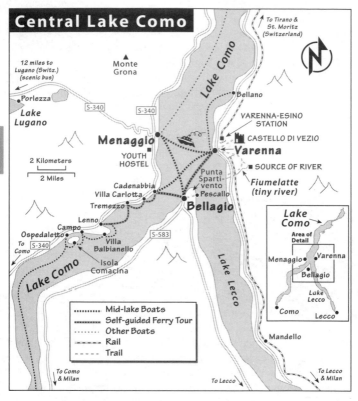

Central Lake Como

To Tirano &
St. Moritz
(Switzerland)

N

Lake Como

12 miles to
Lugano (Switz.)
(scenic bus)

Monte
Grona

Bellano

Porlezza

Lake
Lugano

S-340

S-340

VARENNA-ESINO
STATION

CASTELLO DI VEZIO

Menaggio

YOUTH
HOSTEL

Varenna

2 Kilometers

SOURCE OF RIVER

2 Miles

Punta
Sparti-
vento

Fiumelatte
(tiny river)

Cadenabbia
Villa Carlotta

Pescallo

Tremezzo

Bellagio

Lenno

Campo

Lake
Como

Ospedaletto

S-583

Area of
Detail

To
Como

S-340

Villa
Balbianello

Menaggio

Varenna

Isola
Comacina

Bellagio

Lake Como

Lake
Lecco

*Lake
Lecco*

Como

Lecco

.... Mid-lake Boats
━━━━━ Self-guided Ferry Tour
·········· Other Boats
▭▭▭▭ Rail
------ Trail

Mandello

To Como
& Milan

To Lecco

To Lecco
& Milan

gio) is via the train to Varenna. Once here, limit your activities to the scenic mid-lake area (Varenna and Bellagio).

Here are the specifics: Leaving from Milan's central train station, catch a train heading for Sondrio or Tirano—sometimes the departure board also says "Lecco/Tirano." (Tirano is often confused with Torino...wrong city. And, if you're heading for Varenna, be sure you don't accidentally catch a train to Verona.) All Sondrio-bound trains stop in Varenna, as noted in the fine print on the *partenze* (departures) schedule posted at Milan's train station. Trains leave Milan about every one to two hours (€6.40, 1 hour, likely schedule—but confirm these times: 6:20, 7:20, 8:20, 9:20, 10:20, 12:20, 14:20, 16:20, 17:20, 19:20, 20:20, and 21:20; railpasses accepted). Get a second-class ticket, since first-class wagons are rare on the Sondrio-Tirano route. If you plan to head back to Milan on the train, also buy a return ticket—Varenna's station has no ticket office or ticket machine (though it does have a travel agency that sells train tickets). Stamp the ticket in the yellow box at the front of the tracks or risk a €50 fine. If you run into a problem or need to validate your railpass at Milan's train station, find the helpful Trenitalia Customer Care office in front of track 21 (daily 6:00-24:00).

Leaving Milan, sit on the left for maximum lake-view beauty. Get off at Varenna-Esino. Even though train schedules list only Varenna, Varenna-Esino is what you'll see at the platform—same place.

Long trains serve Varenna's tiny station and stop only briefly. Know what time you're supposed to arrive in Varenna, so you can be ready to disembark with luggage in hand. Because trains can be longer than the station, your car may actually stop before or after the platform. Look out the window. If even part of the train is at the station, you'll need to get out and walk. Tips: Board midtrain to land next to a platform. Leave from the door through which you entered, since you know it's working. You may have to open the train door yourself: If necessary, pull hard on the red handle to open the door.

From Varenna's train station, follow the signs for the ferry boat. Once you reach the ferry dock, walk up to the main road to avoid carting your luggage across the cobblestones that line the lakeside promenade. A taxi from the station costs about €9.

By Train from Milan's Airports: It's a two-step process: First, take the Malpensa Express train from Malpensa Airport or the Starfly bus from Linate Airport to Milan's central train station, then transfer to a Varenna-bound train (described earlier).

By Boat via Como: For a less convenient, much slower, but more scenic trip, you can also get to Varenna from Milan via the town of Como (or vice versa). Trains take you from Milan to Como (hourly, 30-90 minutes). It's a 10-minute walk to the dock, where you catch either the speedy hydrofoil or the leisurely *battello* (slow boat—great for enjoying the scenery) for the ride up the lake to Varenna (slow boat: 3/day, €11.60, 2 hours, last departure about 15:00; hydrofoil: 5/day Mon-Sat, 2/day Sun, €16.20, 1 hour, last departure about 19:00).

By Taxi: A taxi costs roughly €130-165 between Varenna and downtown Milan or Milan's airports.

By Car: In Varenna, the easiest (though most expensive) option for parking is the new multilevel lot at the end of town, across from Villa Monastero (€2/hour, €20/24 hours). Save yourself the time and headache of looking for public parking (described next), and just park in the garage.

In town, you can look for the color-coded lines to decipher the parking options: White is free anytime; yellow is for residents only; and blue means you pay (look for signs, €2/hour, payment times vary during holidays and high season—often Mon-Fri 8:00-20:00, daily in Aug, otherwise free). Buy tickets from meters or at Albergo

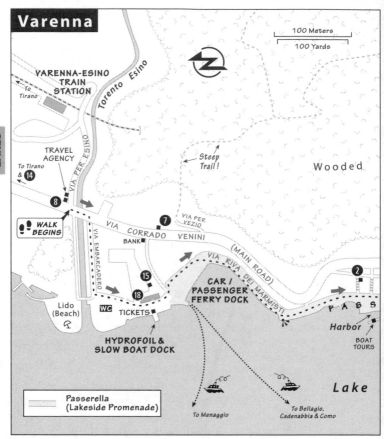

LAKES

Beretta. Leave the ticket on your dashboard; overnight until 8:00 is OK. Parking on the main square is for residents only.

At the train station, parking is free Monday-Friday, but you'll have to pay on Saturdays and Sundays during high season and every day in August (8:00-19:00, feed coins into meter in center of lot and put printed ticket on dashboard).

If you park elsewhere in town and aren't sure if your spot is legal, check with your hotelier.

Getting Around Varenna

Varenna is small, and everything is within a 15-minute walk (except for the Eremo Gaudio hotel). If you'd prefer a taxi, you'll find them waiting at the train station and dock. From either arrival point, a taxi should charge about €9 for a ride to your hotel.

By Taxi: Reliable **Marco Barili** (or his wife Nelly) will meet you at the train station if you know your exact arrival time in Va-

1. Hotel du Lac
2. Albergo Milano & Ristorante la Vista
3. Villa Cipressi & Ristorante la Contrada
4. To Eremo Gaudio
5. Albergo/Ristorante del Sole
6. Villa Elena
7. Hotel/Rist. Montecodeno
8. Albergo Beretta
9. Ristorante il Cavatappi
10. Varennamonamour
11. Osteria Quatro Pass
12. Nilus Bar & Bar il Molo
13. Gelateria Riva
14. To Ristorante il Caminetto & Cooking Course
15. Pub l'Orso
16. Ristorante Isola Nuova
17. Vecchia Varenna
18. Hotel/Ristorante Olivedo
19. Grocery Stores (2)
20. Ornithology & Natural Science Museum; Proloco Info Point
21. Laundry
22. Barilott (Train Tickets)
23. Villa Monastero Entrance

renna. Look for a flashing sign with your name on it. He can also get you to Milan and its airports and, unlike other drivers, he doesn't add surcharges for baggage or early/late departures (€135 to central Milan or Linate Airport, €150 to Malpensa Airport for up to 4 people—or €210 for 5-8 passengers in a minibus, €130 to Bergamo's Orio al Serio Airport, tel. 0341-815-061, taxi.varenna@ tiscali.it).

Helpful Hints

Train Tickets: I Viaggi del Tivano travel agency, Barilott, and Albergo Beretta are the only places in town that sell train tickets to Milan; no tickets are sold at the small train station.

Money: One bank is near Varenna's main square; another is located inland from the boat dock. Both have ATMs (see town map).

Internet Access: Try **Barilott,** which also sells some train and local bus tickets, fresh *panini,* and wines by the glass (Internet access—€4/hour, free for customers, Mon-Sat 7:00-20:00, closed Sun, Via IV Novembre 6, tel. 0341-815-045, Claudia and Fabrizio).

Post Office: It's just off the main square (Tue, Thu, and Sat 8:00-13:00).

Laundry: Lavanderia Pensa Barbara can wash and dry your laundry within 24 hours (€3.50/kilo—about 2 pounds, no self-service, Mon-Fri 9:00-12:00 & 15:00-19:30, Sat 9:00-12:30, closed Sun, Via Venini 31, tel. 0341-830-478, mobile 340-466-2977).

Travel Agency: For bus and boat tours, consider Varenna's travel agency, **I Viaggi del Tivano,** next to Albergo Beretta, a block below the train station. They book planes, trains, and automobiles, and can offer half-day and daylong tours of the region and into Switzerland from April through September (book tours by noon the day before; open Mon-Fri 9:00-18:30, Sat 9:00-16:00, closed Sun, shorter hours off-season, can book rental cars here but pick up in Lecco, no service charge for regional train tickets, €5 service charge for long-distance train tickets, Via Esino 3, tel. 0341-814-009, www.tivanotours.com, info@tivanotours.com, helpful Cristina and Eleonora).

Self-Guided Walk

Welcome to Varenna

Since you came here to relax, this short walk gives you just the town basics.

Bridge Just Below Train Station: This main bridge spans the tiny Esino River, which divides two communities: Perledo (which sprawls up the hill—notice the church spire high above) and the old fishing town of Varenna (huddled around its harbor). The train station, called Varenna-Esino, is named for a third community that sits eight miles higher in the hills.

Cross the bridge and follow the river down to the small square, which hosts a market on Wednesdays. The town's public beach (or *lido*) is just over the cute pedestrian bridge (€2 entry). The inn facing the ferry dock, Hotel Olivedo, has greeted ferry travelers since the 19th century and is named for the olive groves you can see growing halfway up the hill. Natives claim this is the farthest north that olives grow in Europe.

• *Across from Hotel Olivedo is Varenna's...*

Ferry Landing: Since the coming of the train in 1892, Varenna has been *the* convenient access point from "mid-lake" (the communities of Bellagio, Menaggio, and Varenna) to Milan. From this viewpoint, you can almost see how Lake Como is shaped like a man. The head is the north end (to the right, up by the Swiss Alps). Varenna is the man's left hip (to the east). Menaggio, across the lake, is the right hip (to the west). And Bellagio (hiding behind the smaller wooded hill to your left) is the crotch—or, more poetically, Punta Spartivento ("Point that Divides the Wind"). In a more colorful description, a traditional poem says, "Lake Como is a man, with Colico the head, Lecco and Como the feet, and Bellagio the testicles." (In the regional dialect, this rhymes—ask a native to say it for you.)

The farthest ridges high above the right hip mark the border of Switzerland. This region's longtime poverty shaped the local character (much like the Great Depression shaped the outlook of a generation of Americans). Many still remember that this side of the lake was the poorest, because those on the Menaggio side controlled the lucrative cigarette-smuggling business over the Swiss border. Today, the entire region is thriving—thanks to tourism.

• *Walk past the ferry dock toward a small playground, to Varenna's elevated shoreline walk, called the...*

Passerella: A generation ago, Varenna built this elegant lakeside promenade, which connects the ferry dock with the old town

center. Strolling this lane, you'll come to the tiny, two-dinghy, concrete breakwater of a villa. Lake Como is lined with swanky 19th-century villas; their front doors face the lake to welcome visitors arriving by boat. At this point, the modern *passerella* cuts between this villa's water gate and its private harbor. From here, enjoy a good Varenna town view. These buildings are stringently protected by preservation laws; you can't even change the color of your villa's paint.

Just over the hump (which allows boats into a covered moorage), look up at another typical old villa—with a private *passerella*, a lovely veil of wisteria, and a prime lakeview terrace. Many of these villas are owned by the region's "impoverished nobility." They were bred and raised not to work and, therefore, are now unable to pay for the upkeep of their sprawling houses. Lately, these villas are being bought by the region's nouveau riche.

• *At the community harbor, walk to the end of the pier for a town overview, then continue under the old-time arcades toward the multihued homes facing the harbor.*

Varenna Harborfront: There are no streets in the old town—just the characteristic stepped lanes called *contrade*. Varenna was originally a fishing community. Even today, old-timers enjoy Lake Como's counterpart to Norwegian lutefisk: *missoltino*, air-dried

LAKES

and salted lake "sardines." They're served with the region's polenta (different from Venice's, because buckwheat is mixed in with the corn).

Imagine the harbor 200 years ago—busy with coopers expertly fitting chestnut and oak staves into barrels, stoneworkers carving the black marble that was quarried just above town, and fishing boats dragged onto the sloping beach. The little stone harbor dates from about 1600. Today, the fishing boats are just for recreation, and residents gather here with their kids to relax by the lake.

At the south end of the harbor (across from the recommended Bar il Molo *gelateria*), belly up to the banister of the terrace for a colorful town view. Another traditional ditty goes, "If you love Lake Como, you know Bellagio is the pearl...but Varenna is the diamond."

• *Continue straight, leaving the harbor. A lane curves around Hotel du Lac (its fine lakeside terrace welcomes even non-guests for a drink), finishing with an unexpected hill. Finally you'll reach the tiny pebbly town beach below. From here, climb the stairs and go through the yellow arch to the square, called...*

Piazza San Giorgio: Several churches face Varenna's town square. The main church (Chiesa di San Giorgio) dates from the 13th century. Romantic Varenna is an understandably popular spot for weddings—rice often litters the church's front yard. Stepping inside, you'll find a few humble but centuries-old bits of carving and frescoes. The black floor and chapels are made from the local marble.

Across from the square, to the right of the municipal building, is the Proloco Varenna Information Point (TI) and the Ornithology and Natural Science Museum, with its small collection of stuffed birds and other wildlife (open April-Sept, Sat-Sun only).

The Hotel Royal Victoria, also on the main square, recalls the 1839 visit of Queen Victoria, who registered herself as the Countess of Clare in an attempt to remain anonymous.

The trees in the square are planted to make a V for Varenna. The street plan survives from Roman times, when gutters flowed down to the lake. The little church on the lake side of the square is the baptistery. Dating from the ninth century, it's one of the oldest churches on the lake, but is rarely open for visits.

Your walk is over. Facing the church, you can head right to

visit the gardens or hike up to the castle (both described later, under "Sights in Varenna"); left to go to the train station or ferry dock; or back downhill to enjoy the beach (take either of the lanes flanking the Hotel Royal Victoria down to the water).

Sights in Varenna

Castle

A steep and stony trail leads to Varenna's ruined hilltop castle, Castello di Vezio, located in a peaceful, traffic-free, one-chapel town. Take the small road, Via per Vezio (about 100 feet south of—and to the right of—Hotel Montecodeno), and figure on a 20-minute walk one-way. The castle is barren, but enlivened by occasional art exhibits and a falconry-training center.

Cost and Hours: €6, April-Sept Mon-Fri 10:00-18:00, Sat-Sun 10:00-19:00, March and Oct closes one hour earlier, closed Nov-Feb and in bad weather, low-key falconry shows usually around 15:30, but check website or call in morning for times, bar and restaurant at entrance, dinner by reservation only, mobile 333-448-5975, www.castellodivezio.it, info@castellodivezio.it, Nicola.

Gardens

Two separate manicured lakeside gardens—the terraces of Villa  Cipressi and the adjacent, more open grounds of Villa Monastero—are open to the public. Formerly a noble residence, Villa Monastero, filled with overly ornate furnishings from the late 1800s, is also open to the public as a museum.

Cost and Hours: Villa Cipressi—€4, May-Nov daily 8:00-18:00, closed Dec-April; Villa Monastero—gardens-€5, gardens and museum-€8; gardens open March-Oct daily 9:00-18:00, until 19:00 May-Sept, closed Nov-Feb; museum open March-April and Oct daily 9:00-18:00, May-Sept Mon-Thu & Sat-Sun 9:00-19:00, Fri 9:00-14:00, closed Nov-Feb; bar in garden serves snacks, tel. 0341-295-450, www.villamonastero.eu.

Swimming

There are three spots to swim in Varenna: the free little beach behind the Hotel Royal Victoria off Piazza San Giorgio, the central lakefront area by Nilus Bar, and the *lido*. The *lido* is by far the best-equipped for swimmers. Just north of the boat dock, it's essentially a wide concrete slab with sand and a swimming area off an old boat ramp. It has showers, bathrooms, a restaurant, a bar, and lounge chairs for rent (entry-€2, umbrellas-€4, lounge chairs-€6, tel.

0341-815-3700). Swimming by the boat dock is strictly forbidden for safety reasons.

Boat Tours
Taxi Boat Varenna organizes hour-long central lake tours (€30/person), 30-minute "Varenna seen from the water" tours (€10/person), and 50-minute romantic private tours (€150/couple). Ask Luca about his special "Tour George"; book direct on their website (April-Oct, mobile 349-229-0953, www.taxiboatlecco.com, info@taxiboatlecco.com). A similar company works out of Bellagio.

Near Varenna
▲▲Self-Guided Ferry Tour: Lake Como
The best simple day out is to take the *battello navetta* (mid-lake

ferry) on its entire 50-minute Varenna-Bellagio-Cadenabbia-Villa Carlotta-Tremezzo-Lenno route. On the return trip, stop at any sights that interest you (Lenno to see Villa del Balbianello, Tremezzo for Villa Carlotta, and/or Bellagio). This commentary describes what you'll see along the way.

Leaving Varenna: Looking back at Varenna from the lake, you'll see the castle rising above the town, with new Varenna on the

left (bigger buildings and modern ferry dock), and old Varenna on the right (tighter, more colorful buildings). The big development high on the hillside is an ugly example of cronyism (without the mayor involved, this would never have happened). Under the castle is a grove of olives (reputedly the northernmost ones grown in Italy). Because the lake is protected from the north wind, exotic flowers grow well in the lake's many fine gardens. To the right of Varenna's castle are the town cemetery, a lift up to the Eremo Gaudio hotel (a former hermitage), and a spurt of water gushing out of the mountain just above lake level. This is the tiny Fiumelatte, Italy's shortest river.

Mid-Lake: The Swiss Alps rise to the north. Across the lake is Menaggio, and just over the ridge from that are Lugano and the "Swiss Riviera." The winds alternate between north and south. In pre-industrial times, traders harnessed the wind to sail up and down the lake. Notice the V-shaped, fjord-like terrain. Lake Como is glacier-cut. And, at more than 1,200 feet deep, it's Europe's deepest lake. You'll cruise past the Punta Spartivento, the point that literally "splits the wind," and where the two "legs" of the lake join (Lake Lecco is on the left/east, and Lake Como on the right).

Approaching Bellagio: Survey the park to the left of Punta Spartivento—it's a pleasant walk from town. Bellagio has three

times the number of hotel rooms as Varenna, as you can see upon approach. The town, with its strip of swanky hotels, is bookended by Villa Serbelloni (five stars) on the left, dominating the lakefront, and the sprawling Grand Hotel Bretagne (four stars) on the right. In the 19th century, aristocratic

Russians hung out in the Serbelloni, and well-heeled English chose the Bretagne. These days, the Serbelloni is the second-most-luxurious hotel on the lake after Villa d'Este, while Bretagne is mired in a long renovation project.

Approaching Cadenabbia: From Bellagio, you cross the lake to Cadenabbia. Above Cadenabbia, the Church of St. Martin seems stranded halfway up the mountain. This side of the lake has nearly all the area's traffic, thanks to a big road that ended up separating many fine lakefront gardens from their villas. Farther north is the village of Dongo, where Mussolini and his girlfriend were captured in the last months of World War II as they tried to escape into Switzerland. They were shot here on the lake, and their bodies were hung ingloriously in Milan for public viewing.

Villa Carlotta: Because of lake taxes and high maintenance costs, owners of once-elite villas have been forced to turn them

into hotels or to open their doors to the paying public. This is an example of the latter. One of the finest properties on the lake, Villa Carlotta is most visited for its Canova statue and lush garden.

Tremezzo: Notice the Grand Hotel Tremezzo, with its striking Liberty-style (Art Nouveau) facade and swimming pool floating on the lake. Above the town is a villa built in the 19th-century Romantic Age to resemble a medieval castle. After the Tremezzo stop (just before the Tremezzo church), you'll see a fine public park with a fountain. When the road separated this land from its villa, its owners gave it to the community. Here the lake is dotted by a string of fine old villas with elegant landings and gated boathouses. Built in the days before motors, they are now too small for most modern lake boats. Tullio Abbate is famous in this area for building speedy, high-end lake boats.

Lenno: This is your last stop. About 400 yards farther along the shore is a tiny dock for shuttle boats headed for Villa del Balbianello (of *Star Wars: Episode II* and *Casino Royale* fame).

Sailing Home: Get off the boat at Lenno; from here you can return to Bellagio or Varenna, stopping along the way as you like.

Hiking

The town of Fiumelatte, about a half-mile south of Varenna, was named for its "milky river." It's the shortest river in Italy (at 800 feet) and runs—like most of the area tourist industry—only from April through September (though even then it may be dry, depending on the weather). The *La Sorgente del Fiumelatte* brochure, available at Varenna's travel agency, lays out a walk from Varenna to the Fiumelatte, then to the castle, and back. It's a 30-minute hike to the source *(sorgente)* of the river (at Varenna's monastery, take the high road, drop into the tranquil and evocative cemetery, and climb steps to the wooded trail leading to the peaceful and refreshing cave from which the river spouts).

For a longer hike in the opposite direction with lake views, ask the travel agency about the Wayfarers' Path (hike one-way up the lake, about 1.5 hours, not quite as steep as Fiumelatte hike). You can return by train from Bellano (€1.30, Bellano not included on mid-lake pass, check schedule before you go), or take the ferry to Menaggio and catch a connecting boat back to Varenna.

▲Cooking Course

Chef Moreno of the recommended Ristorante il Caminetto picks you up in Varenna, zips you up the mountain to his restaurant (experience Italian driving!), and then teaches you some basics of Italian cooking. Learn how to handcraft fresh pasta or prep regional specialties. Classes last about three hours, plus time to *mangiare*. People love the experience and find Moreno a charming teacher and host (€50 includes trip, lesson, recipes, and lunch complete with wine, cookies, and coffee; Mon, Tue, Thu, and Fri; 10:00 pickup from Varenna landing, return by 16:00, reservations mandatory, tel. 0341-815-225, www.ilcaminettoonline.com, info@ilcaminettoonline.com).

Sleep Code

(€1 = about $1.30, country code: 39)
S = Single, **D** = Double/Twin, **T** = Triple, **Q** = Quad, **b** = bathroom, **s** = shower only. Unless otherwise noted, credit cards are accepted, English is spoken, and breakfast is included. Varenna, like many cities in Italy, charges a tourist tax (€1 per person per night, must be paid in cash at check-out).

To help you sort easily through these listings, I've divided the accommodations into three categories based on the price for a standard double room with bath:

  $$$ **Higher Priced**—Most rooms €150 or more.
   $$ **Moderately Priced**—Most rooms between €100-150.
    $ **Lower Priced**—Most rooms €100 or less.

Prices can change without notice; verify the hotel's current rates online or by email. For the best prices, always book direct.

Sleeping in Varenna

Reservations are tight in August, snug May through October, and wide open most of the rest of the year. Many places close in winter. High-season prices are listed here; prices get soft off-season (Nov-April).

$$$ Hotel du Lac, filling a refined and modernized 19th-century villa, is the finest hotel in town. From its exclusive private perch on the point, it offers a quiet lakefront breakfast terrace, generous public spaces; a friendly, professional staff; and 16 delightful rooms—all but 3 with lake views (standard Db-€195, bigger Db-€250, these high-season prices are for May-mid-Oct, €20 less in shoulder season, closed Nov-March, air-con, free Wi-Fi, parking-€16, Via del Prestino 11, tel. 0341-830-238, www.albergodulac.com, info@albergodulac.com).

$$$ Albergo Milano, located right in the old town, is graciously run by Egidio and his Swiss wife, Bettina. Fusing the best of Italy with the best of Switzerland, this well-run, romantic hotel has eight comfortable rooms with extravagant views, balconies, or big terraces (Sb-€125, Db-€150-170, €10 extra for view terrace, €5/day cash discount, closed mid-Nov-Feb, no elevator, free Wi-Fi; from the station, take main road to town and turn right at steep alley where sidewalk and guardrail break; Via XX Settembre 35, tel. 0341-830-298, www.varenna.net, hotelmilano@varenna.net). This place whispers *luna di miele*—honeymoon (see website for 3-night honeymoon deal). Nearby is **$$ Casa Rossa,** an annex with six comfortable rooms and two apartments that work well for families (Db-€135-165, proportionately more for third or fourth person, breakfast served at main hotel). Their recommended Ristorante la Vista is worth considering for dinner.

$$ Villa Cipressi is a sprawling, centuries-old lakeside mansion with 33 warmly outfitted, modern rooms. Its public spaces are often busy with wedding parties. Rooms without views face the street and can be noisy. The villa sits in a huge, quiet terraced garden that non-guests pay to see (Sb-€140, non-view Db-€170, view Db-€195, extra cot-€40, extra bed-€60, ask for Rick Steves discount, elevator, guest computer, free Wi-Fi, garden access, Via IV Novembre 22, tel. 0341-830-113, www.hotelvillacipressi.it, info@hotelvillacipressi.it, Davide).

$$ Eremo Gaudio stands out with a commanding lake view high above Varenna. Once an orphanage, it became a hermitage run by the Catholic Church, and then—since 2000—a modern hotel accessed by a private funicular. Perfect for monks with champagne tastes, it's peaceful, with awe-inspiring view balconies and a breakfast terrace. Thirteen bright, plain-but-comfy rooms climb up the main building, and 15 less dramatic but equally comfortable rooms huddle below at the foot of the funicular. Suppers are served on the terrace (upper rooms: Sb-€110, Db-€130, Db with balcony-€148; lower rooms: Db-€120-148; closed Nov-Feb, all rooms have lake views, air-con May-Oct, requires walking up steep hills and steps—taking a taxi from station is recommended, quarter-mile south of Varenna's main square at Via Roma 25, tel. 0341-815-301, www.eremogaudio.it, eremogaudio@yahoo.it).

$$ Albergo del Sole is a no-frills hotel over a restaurant right on the town square. Run by fun-loving Enzo, the hotel has eight comfy rooms and no hint of a lake view (Sb-€90; Db-€130, €105 off-season; fans, hardwood floors, shiny bathrooms, elevator, free Wi-Fi, Piazza San Giorgio 17, tel. 0341-815-218, www.albergodelsolevarenna.it, albergo.sole@virgilio.it).

$ Villa Elena, a grandmotherly, low-energy place on the main square, offers a tranquil rest and the best budget beds in town. English-speaking Signora Seta ("Silk") Vitali, who lives downstairs, rents three characteristic, antique-filled rooms that all share one bathroom and an updated kitchen/dining room with a view terrace. With only twin beds, it's not for romantics, but it is a great value (D-€70, cash only, no breakfast, it's the house with the vine-covered pergola at Piazza San Giorgio 7 near Via San Giovanni, tel. 0341-830-575, www.villaelenavarenna.it, info@villaelenavarenna.it).

$ Albergo Beretta, on the main road a block below the station, has 10 pleasant rooms, several with balconies (and street noise). Second-floor rooms are quietest. This place, above a coffee shop that doubles as the reception, feels homey but lacks any lakeside glamour (D-€60, Db-€70, larger room-€80, extra bed-€12, breakfast-€6 but free with 2-night stay and this book, no elevator, Via per Esino 1, tel. 0341-830-132, hotelberetta@iol.it).

$ Hotel Montecodeno, with 11 decent rooms and no views, is a functional concrete box just off the main road between the train station and lake (Sb-€80, Db-€105, extra bed-€10, air-con, guest computer and free Wi-Fi, attached restaurant serves fresh fish and a €23 "Rick Steves" fixed-price meal if you show this book beforehand; if you stay 3 nights and pay cash, you get 1 meal included per guest or a 15 percent cash discount—take your pick; Via della Croce 2, tel. 0341-830-123, www.hotelmontecodeno.com, info@hotelmontecodeno.com, kind Marina Castelli and Lucia).

Eating in Varenna

Dining with a Lake View

Ristorante la Vista, at Albergo Milano, feels like a private hotel restaurant but also welcomes non-guests. On a balmy evening, their terrace overlooking the town and the lake is hard to beat. Egidio (or Egi—pronounced "edgy") and his staff give traditional cuisine a creative twist, and his selection is great for foodies with discerning tastes. I'd go with his €38 three-course fixed-price dinner (Mon and Wed-Sat 19:00-22:00, closed Sun and Tue, reservations required, Via XX Settembre 35, tel. 0341-830-298).

Ristorante la Contrada, with its terrace-side location, is run by the Villa Cipressi and takes advantage of the villa's elegant garden, trickling fountain, and lake view. Indoor seating glows with a warm and romantic air, and the garden is a delight on warm summer evenings. Fresh daily specialties and professional service make this a worthwhile splurge. However, weddings and conference groups can crowd the place and distract from the service (€40 meals plus wine, daily 12:30-14:00 & 19:15-21:30, may close for weddings, Via IV Novembre 22, tel. 0341-830-113).

Dining Without a Lake View

Ristorante il Cavatappi, a tiny place on a quiet lane just off the town square, serves old-time specialties, such as spaghetti with *missoltino,* the air-dried lake fish that natives like more than tourists do. Helpful owner-chef Mario is happy to be considered a lunatic gourmet. With just five tables, he can connect personally with diners. Talk with him, make a plan, then let him loose. Plan on spending €28-38 plus wine (daily 12:30-14:30 & 19:30-21:45, reservations recommended for dinner, Via XX Settembre 10, tel. 0341-815-349).

Varennamonamour, an upscale eatery hiding just up from the water, is popular with fashionable Italians. Its seasonal menu has a nouvelle cuisine flair, with a few popular mainstays fresh from the lake. The cream-and-brown modern decor harmonizes well with the original exposed stone walls to create a classy, welcoming space (€13-15 pastas, €13-18 *secondi*, hours/days can vary—generally daily in high season, Contrada Scoscesa 7, tel. 033-181-4016).

Osteria Quatro Pass is a welcoming bistro known for its homemade pasta and fish. It offers 14 candlelit tables under picturesque vaults, plus sidewalk seating (€12-20 pastas, €10-20 *secondi*, daily 12:00-14:00 & 19:00-22:00, closed Wed outside of peak season, Via XX Settembre 20, tel. 0341-815-091, Lollo).

Eating Simply on the Harbor

The harborfront is lined with several simple eateries, all with great lakefront seating.

Nilus Bar, with a young waitstaff, serves crêpes, pizzas, big mixed salads, hot sandwiches, soup of the day, and cocktails with a smile (Wed-Mon 12:00-22:30, hours can vary and bar open longer, closed Tue and Dec-Feb, cash only, tel. 0341-815-228, Fulvia and Giovanni).

Bar il Molo, next door, is good for a casual meal on the harbor or a gelato with a view (€9-10 pizzas, €7-9 pastas, €5-8 salads, €6 toasted sandwiches, daily 11:00-24:00, closed Nov-March, tel. 0341-830-070). They also have a room full of gifty edibles for sale.

At **Gelateria Riva,** you can get a cup or cone to go, then grab a pillowy seat on the bulkhead. Duillo is the only guy in town who prepares his gelato fresh every day. Try his *nocciola* (hazelnut) before making your choice. Ask the day before if you want to watch the gelato being made (daily 12:00-19:00, open later June-Sept, closed off-season).

Eating Simply Without a Lake View

Ristorante del Sole, facing the town square, serves respectable, well-priced meals and Neapolitan-style pizzas. Making few concessions to the tourist crowds, this family-friendly restaurant caters to residents, providing a fun atmosphere, a cozy, walled-in garden in back, and tables on the square (€7-9 pizzas, €6-10 pastas, €10-19 *secondi*, daily 12:00-14:30 & 18:30-22:30, Piazza San Giorgio 21, tel. 0341-815-218).

Ristorante il Caminetto is a homey, backwoods mountain trattoria in Gittana, a tiny town high above Varenna. Getting there entails a curvy 10-minute drive—they'll pick you up for free in Piazza San Giorgio at 19:30, deliver you to the restaurant, and then dish up classic fare at small-town prices. Husband-and-wife team Moreno and Rossella take pride in their specialties, including grilled meats and risotto with porcini mushrooms and berries. This is a good place to set a price and trust your host to bring whatever's best (€16-25 *dégustation* menu, wine extra, Thu-Tue 12:30-14:30 & 19:30-21:30, closed Wed, reservations mandatory to confirm pick-up from Varenna at 19:30, Viale Progresso 6, tel. 0341-815-225 or 0341-815-127, mobile 347-331-2238).

Other Eateries

Pub l'Orso is the hotspot in town for wine or beer and a light meal. Oozing character, it's behind Hotel Olivedo in a renovated shed that used to be a marble-polishing shop (closed Mon). At **Ristorante Montecodeno,** a cozy little place on the big road, chef Ferruccio serves a plate of eight different tasty lake fish specialties (including *missoltino*). **Ristorante Isola Nuova** is a newish restaurant with a fresh atmosphere, buried in the old town with no sea view (closed Tue). The venerable **Vecchia Varenna** is the only classy restaurant actually on the harbor (old place with new management). And at **Hotel Olivedo,** a grand old hotel facing the ferry dock, you can eat in a classic dining hall.

Picnics: Varenna's two little grocery stores have all you need for a tasty balcony or breakwater picnic-dinner. The *salumeria* on the square is best for meats, cheese, and bread; try their homemade salami (Tue-Sat 8:00-12:30 & 16:00-19:30, Sun-Mon 8:00-12:30 only). The store just north of the main square by the pharmacy stocks fresh fruits, veggies, and a few essentials (daily 7:30-12:30, Tue-Sat also 16:00-19:30).

Varenna Connections

Remember, if leaving Varenna by train, you can't purchase tickets at the station. Instead, you can buy them from the travel agency (I Viaggi del Tivano), Albergo Beretta next door, or Barilott just off the main square (see "Helpful Hints," earlier). Stamp your ticket in the yellow machine at the station before boarding. If those places are closed, win the sympathy of the conductor and buy your ticket as soon as you get on board for an additional fee. (Find him before he finds you—or you'll likely be charged an even stiffer penalty.)

Varenna to Milan by Train: Trains leave Varenna for Milano Centrale (1 hour, €6.40, likely schedule for daily and direct trains: 5:36, 6:23, 6:35, 7:37, 8:37, 10:37, 12:37, 14:37, 16:37, 17:37, 18:37, 20:37, 21:37, and 22:21; if you board a train at a time not listed here, it's likely a local milk-run train that will take twice as long).

Varenna to Stresa by Train: Trains run about every two hours (2.75-4 hours, transfer in Milan).

Varenna to St. Moritz in Switzerland by Train: From Varenna, you have easy access to the Bernina Express scenic train to St. Moritz. Note that this is only realistic from April through October. First, take the train to Tirano, and then transfer to the Bernina Express train to St. Moritz (4/day, allow 4-5 hours with transfer; for details see www.rhb.ch). For information and a time-table for this route, stop by the I Viaggi del Tivano travel agency (see "Helpful Hints," earlier), or ask your hotelier for the handy tourist information book produced by local travel agencies. Don't forget your passport for trips into Switzerland.

Bellagio

The self-proclaimed "Pearl of the Lake" is a classy combination of tidiness and Old World elegance. If you don't mind that "tramp

in a palace" feeling, it's a fine place to shop for ties and umbrellas while surrounding yourself with the more adventurous posh travelers. Heavy curtains between the harborfront arcades create welcome shade and keep visitors and their poodles from sweating. Thriving yet still cute, Bellagio is a much more substantial town than Varenna (which has one-third the number of hotel beds and almost no shops).

Orientation to Bellagio

Tourist Information
The TI is right downtown, at the slow boat and hydrofoil dock (April-Oct Mon-Sat 9:00-12:30 & 13:00-18:00, Sun 10:00-14:00; Nov-March shorter hours and closed Tue and Sun; tel. 031-950-204, www.bellagiolakecomo.com).

Arrival in Bellagio
Bellagio is best reached via ferry from Varenna (€4.60); or by ferry, hydrofoil, or slow boat from Como.

By Boat: Bellagio has two docks a few minutes' walk apart. The northern docks are for the passenger-only slow boat (*battello* or *battello navetta*) and the hydrofoil *(servizio rapido)*. The southern dock is for all "ferry boats" *(traghetti):* both the car ferry (cars and foot passengers) and the passenger-only ferry. Ask around to make sure you're waiting at the correct dock. Remember that if you want to know all your departure options beyond Varenna, Cadenabbia, and Menaggio, you need to study four different timetables. Confirm your intentions at the kiosk near either dock.

By Car: Parking is difficult, but you can try for a spot near the lake or in the parking lot at the ferry dock (white lines are always free, yellow lines are for residents only, blue lines cost €1.50/hour—pay with coins in gray or blue machines and stick ticket in car window).

Helpful Hints

Internet Access: Bellagio Point has a slick Internet café, complete with great sandwiches, wine-tasting options, and free Wi-Fi if you buy a drink (€2/30 minutes, daily 10:00-22:00, Salita Plinio 8, tel. 031-950-437, www.bellagiopoint.com). Julio also rents apartments (see "Sleeping in Bellagio," later).

Laundry: La Lavandera is bright and new. Don't be discouraged if it looks closed; the lights come on automatically when you enter (€8.50 wash/dry, open daily 24 hours, Salita Carlo Grandi 21—this street is also marked as Via Specula, tel. 339-410-6852).

Sights in Bellagio

Villa Serbelloni Park

If you need a destination, you can take a guided tour of this park, which overlooks the town. The villa itself, owned by the Rockefeller Foundation, is not open to the public.

Cost and Hours: €9, April-Oct, tours Tue-Sun at 11:00 and 15:30, no tours Mon or when rainy, 1.5 hours, first two-thirds of walk is uphill, show up at the little tour office in the medieval tower on Piazza della Chiesa 15 minutes before tour time to buy tickets, confirm time at office, tel. 031-951-555.

Strolling

Explore the steep-stepped lanes rising from the harborfront. While Johnnie Walker and jewelry sell best at lake level, the natives shop up the hill. Piazza della Chiesa, near the top of town, has a worth-a-look church (with its art described in an English-language handout).

The administrative capital of the mid-lake region, Bellagio is located where the two southern legs of the lake split off. For an easy break in a park with a great view, wander right on out to the crotch. Meander past the rich and famous Hotel Villa Serbelloni, and walk five minutes to Punta Spartivento ("Point

LAKES

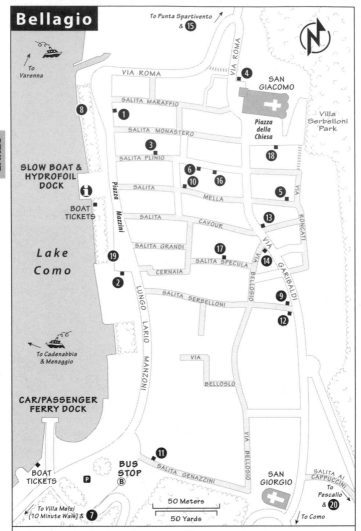

Bellagio

1. Hotel Florence
2. Hotel/Rist./Snack Bar Metropole
3. Hotel Centrale
4. Albergo Europa
5. Bellagio B&B Apartments
6. Il Borgo Apartments
7. To Giardini di Villa Melzi Apartments
8. The Florence Ristorante
9. Trattoria San Giacomo
10. Rist. Terrazza Barchetta
11. Enoteca Cava Turacciolo
12. Aperitivo Et Al
13. Gelateria del Borgo
14. Caligari Alimentari
15. To La Punta Ristorante
16. Internet Café
17. Launderette
18. Villa Serbelloni Park Tickets
19. Bellagio Water-Taxi Lake Tours
20. To Bellagio Water Sports (Kayak Tours)

that Divides the Wind"). You'll find a Renoir atmosphere complete with an inviting bar-restaurant (see "Eating in Bellagio," later), a tiny harbor, and a chance to sit on a park bench and gaze north past Menaggio, Varenna, and the end of the lake to the Swiss Alps.

For another stroll, head south from the car-ferry dock down the tree-shaded promenade. Ten minutes later, you'll pass the town's concrete swimming area. The grassy, pebbly, public San Giovanni beach (no showers) is another 20 minutes farther south from there.

Villa Melzi Gardens
A 10-minute walk south from the ferry dock, this picture-perfect lakeside expanse of exotic plants, flowers, trees, and Neoclassical sculpture was assembled by the vice president of Napoleon's Italian Republic in the early 19th century.

Cost and Hours: €6.50, April-Oct daily 9:30-18:30, last entry at 18:00, closed Nov-March, mobile 339-457-3838, www.giardinidivillamelzi.it.

Hikes and Walks
The TI has free brochures for three well-crafted walking tours, varying from one to three hours, all of which explore the city and environs. Sites include villas, gardens, churches, an old-fashioned dairy shop, medieval towers, and a nautical instruments museum. The TI also sells a hiking map for €3 that shows four different hikes ranging in difficulty and duration.

Bellagio Water-Taxi Lake Tours
With a small stand at the boat docks, Jennine and Luca offer tours and private service in their luxurious and powerful boat. Their basic 2.5-hour tour, guided by Luca, includes a fun hour at mid-lake, with a float-by of Richard Branson's villa, as well as a stop at Villa del Balbianello, where you'll take an English tour.

Cost and Hours: €50, 10 percent discount if you reserve direct and bring this book, price includes entry and tour of villa—worth €13, generally runs at 13:30 but check blackboard for day's offerings or call, mobile 338-524-4914, www.bellagiowatertaxis.com, bellagiowatertaxis@gmail.com.

Bellagio Water Sports
Friendly Michele offers kayaking tours within a 10-minute walk of the town center. His popular 1.5- and 2-hour tours cover the Bellagio coast, while his 3-hour tour includes a stop at Villa Melzi. He also rents kayaks for those willing to go solo.

Cost and Hours: €25/1.5-hour tour, €30/2-hour tour, €35/3-hour tour; kayak rentals €15/1.5 hours, €17.50/2 hours, €22.50/3 hours; no tours on Sun, located on Pescallo Bay at via Sfondrati 1 near Hotel La Pergola, mobile 340-394-9375, www.bellagiowatersports.com, info@bellagiowatersports.com.

Sleeping in Bellagio

This is a "boom or bust" lake resort, with high-season prices (those listed here) straight through from May to September, plus a brief shoulder season (with discounted prices) in April and from October to November. Off-season (Dec-March), nearly everything is closed down.

$$$ Hotel Florence has a prime lakefront setting in the center of town. The 150-year-old, family-run place features 30 rooms, hardwood floors, bold earth tones, and a rich touch of Old World elegance (Sb-€125, Db-€145-210, Db suite-€150-270, prices depend on view and balcony, closed Nov-March, fans available on request, handheld showers, elevator, free Wi-Fi, Piazza Mazzini 46, tel. 031-950-342, www.hotelflorencebellagio.it, info@hotelflorencebellagio.it, run by the Austrian Ketzlar family).

$$$ Hotel Metropole, dominating Bellagio's waterfront between the ferry docks, is a grand old place with plush public spaces. Its modern rooms have all the comforts, but with a bit of an institutional feel. Many of its 42 rooms have lake views (Sb-€120, €140 with balcony, Db-€160, €190 with balcony, €220 with terrace, air-con, elevator, free Wi-Fi, stunning roof terrace, Piazza Mazzini 1, tel. 031-950-409, www.albergometropole.it, info@albergometropole.it).

$$ Hotel Centrale, managed with pride and care by Giacomo Borelli, warmly welcomes its guests into a true-blue family operation: Signore Borelli's two sons help out, his mama painted the art, and grandpa crafted much of the Art Deco-era furniture. This place has generous public spaces and many thoughtful touches—and its 17 comfortable rooms are a great value, even without lake views (Sb-€110, Db-€130, €5/night discount with this book, air-con, elevator, guest computer, free Wi-Fi, Salita Plinio 7, tel. 031-951-940, www.hc-bellagio.com, info@hc-bellagio.com).

$ Albergo Europa, run with low energy, is in a concrete annex behind a restaurant, away from the waterfront. Its 10 rooms have no charm but are comfortable (Sb-€60, Db-€80, no elevator, free parking, Via Roma 21, tel. 031-950-471, www.hoteleuropabellagio.it, info@hoteleuropabellagio.it, Marchesi family).

$ Bellagio B&B Apartments, with three units for rent, are located behind the *gelateria* at the top of town. Julio also runs the Bellagio Point Internet café, which serves as the reception (Db-€60, more for additional people, 2-night minimum, no breakfast, free Wi-Fi, reception at Salita Plinio 8, apartments at Salita Cavour 37, tel. 031-951-680, www.bellagiobedandbreakfast.com, info@bellagiobedandbreakfast.com). Julio also has five large apartments a 15-minute walk from Bellagio (toward Como, Db-€80-100 for 4 people).

$ Il Borgo Apartments rents seven modern *Better Homes and Gardens*-quality apartments with kitchenettes in the old center at great prices. Easygoing Flavio is available for check-in daily 9:00-12:00, or by appointment (Db-€100, 2 bigger apartments for up to 6 people-€120, cash discount, no breakfast, 3-night minimum required, air-con, Wi-Fi, Salita Plinio 4, tel. 031-952-497, mobile 338-193-5559, www.borgoresidence.it, info@borgoresidence.it).

$ Giardini di Villa Melzi Apartments provides modern lodgings in three double bedrooms and three studios with kitchenettes in the little harbor of Loppia, about a 15-minute walk south of Bellagio. A free pass allows guests to take a shortcut to Bellagio through the Villa Melzi Gardens (€50/person, usually 3-night minimum—ask, guest computer, free parking, Via Melzi d'Eril 23, tel. 339-221-4394, www.bellagiowelcome.com, info@bellagiowelcome.com, Ornella).

Eating in Bellagio

On the Lakefront

These places (also listed under "Sleeping in Bellagio," earlier) offer wonderful lakeside tables and, considering the setting, reasonable prices.

Hotel Metropole Ristorante, while a mediocre food value, has a full menu and is a relaxing delight with good service (€12-16 pastas, €14-22 *secondi*, April-Oct daily 12:00-14:30 & 19:00-21:30, closed Nov-March, Piazza Mazzini 1, tel. 031-950-409) **Hotel Metropole Snack Bar,** next to the restaurant, is quite good, with simple €9 pastas and sandwiches and fine €7-12 salads (April-Oct daily 12:00-21:30, bar open later, closed Nov-March, good service, great locale).

The Florence is nicely situated under a trellis of flowers across from the Florence Hotel, away from the ferry fumes. This is a lovely perch for a drink or meal (€16 pastas, €22 *secondi*, simpler lunch menu of salads and lighter fare, April-Sept daily 12:00-14:30 & 19:00-22:00, bar open all day).

In the Old Town, Without Lake Views

Trattoria San Giacomo is a high-energy place that's respected for its traditional cuisine, such as *riso e filetto di pesce* (rice and perch fillet in butter and sage). It has daily seasonal specials and an inviting €25 fixed-price meal based on regional specialties. Choose between fun seating on a steep, cobbled lane or tight seating inside (Mon and Wed-Thu 12:00-14:30 & 19:00-21:30, Fri-Sun open later midday and evenings, closed Tue and Dec-Feb, Salita Serbelloni 45, tel. 031-950-329, Aurelio).

Ristorante Terrazza Barchetta, set on a terrace with no lake view and bedecked with summery colors, puts a creative twist on regional favorites such as lake fish. Don't confuse it with the street-level bar-trattoria—head up the stairs to the second floor. Reservations are recommended (€15 pastas, €20 *secondi*, Wed-Mon 12:00-14:30 & 19:00-22:30, closed Tue, Salita Mella 13, tel. 031-951-389).

Other Options

Wine-Tasting: Step into the vaulted stone cellar of the funky **Enoteca Cava Turacciolo** to taste three regional wines with a sampling of cheeses, meats, and breads (€19/person with this book, Thu-Tue April-Oct 10:30-1:00, Nov-Dec and March 18:00-24:00, closed Wed and Jan-Feb, Salita Genazzini 3, tel. 031-950-975, Norberto and Rosy). **Aperitivo Et Al,** slick and jazzy, is a trendier wine bar, offering mixed *salumi* and *formaggi* plates (€8-12), big fresh salads (€9-12), and light lunches, along with a great selection of wines by the glass (€14-18/three-glass tasting—totaling a half-bottle of wine per person, add antipasto plate for €24, also Super Tuscan wine-tastings, daily 11:30-24:00, closed Dec-Feb and Tue off-season, free Wi-Fi, Salita Serbelloni 34, tel. 031-951-523).

Gelato: Residents agree that you won't find the best *gelateria* in town among the sundaes served on the waterfront. Instead, climb to the top of town to **Gelateria del Borgo** (daily 10:00-22:30, shorter hours off-season, closed Nov-March, Via Garibaldi 46, tel. 031-950-755, Stefania and Gianfranco).

Picnics: You'll find benches at the park, along the waterfront in town, and lining the promenade south of town. Pick up your picnic supplies at **Caligari Alimentari.** They have roast chicken, ribs, and focaccia, and are happy to make fresh sandwiches to order (Tue-Sat 7:30-13:00 & 16:00-19:30, Sun 7:30-13:00, closed Mon, shorter hours off-season, on corner of Via Garibaldi and Via Carlo Bellosio, tel. 031-951-815).

Punta Spartivento: This dramatic natural park, a 10-minute walk north of town, is a great place for either a picnic or a meal at **La Punta Ristorante** (€9 pastas, €13 fish, €22 meat courses, March-Oct daily 12:00-14:30 & 19:00-22:00, bar open 14:30-19:00 for snacks only, closed Nov-Feb, tel. 031-951-888).

Menaggio

Menaggio has more urban bulk than its neighbors, but visitors are charmed by its lovely lakefront park. Since many find Lake

Como too dirty for swimming, consider spending time in Menaggio's fine public pool (look for the *lido*). This is the starting point for a few hikes. (Just a few decades ago, cigarette smugglers used these trails at night to sneak back into Italy from Switzerland with their tax-free booty.) The TI has information about mountain biking and catching the bus to trailheads on nearby Mount Grona. Ask for the free *Walking in the Province of Como* booklet, with information on 18 different walks detailing historical, artistic, and natural features (**TI** in Piazza Garibaldi open Mon-Sat 9:00-12:30 & 14:30-18:00, closed Wed Nov-March, closed Sun year-round, tel. 0344-32-924, www.menaggio.com).

Sleeping in Menaggio

$ La Marianna B&B has eight rooms and a fine restaurant in Cadenabbia, about a mile south of Menaggio on a busy road (Db with view-€98, lakeside terrace at restaurant—guests receive a 25 percent restaurant discount, air-con, tel. 0344-43095, www.la-marianna.com, inn@la-marianna.com, Ty and Paola). The hourly Como-Menaggio bus #C10 stops here, and the ferry dock for mid-lake towns via Bellagio is 300 yards away.

$ La Primula Youth Hostel has a great location on the lake, a two-minute walk from the ferry dock (€20/person in dorm room, Db-€54, family room with bathroom and 4 beds-€80, €2 extra for nonmembers, pizzas from €6, guest computer, Wi-Fi, sailing school, kayak and mountain bike rentals, cooking classes, tel. 0344-32356, www.lakecomohostel.com, info@lakecomohostel.com). The hourly Como-Menaggio bus #C10 stops right by the hostel.

Menaggio Connections

From Menaggio to Milan: It's a 20-minute ferry to Varenna (boats hourly), where trains connect to Milan (every 1-2 hours, 1 hour). More fast trains depart from Como than Varenna. From Menaggio, take hourly local bus #C10 (€3.50, 1-2/hour, 1 hour) to Como, where you can catch the train (hourly, 30-90 minutes). If you need to reach Malpensa Airport, you could take bus #C10 to Como, then take a train to Saronno, which is on the Malpensa Express train line.

From Menaggio to Switzerland: Public bus #C12 departs about every hour or two from Piazza Roma for Lugano (€10 round-trip, 1 hour, buy tickets at bus stop on Via Calvi). In summer, the yellow Palm Express bus runs once daily to **Lugano** (1 hour) and **St. Moritz** (3 hours). Off-season (mid-Oct–mid-June), the bus runs only on weekends. Advance reservations are required (www.post-bus.ch)—and remember to bring your passport.

More Sights on Lake Como

Villa Carlotta

If you plan to tour one of Lake Como's famed villas, this is the best for gardens and flowers (its forte). I see the lakes as a break from Italy's art, but if you're in need of a place that charges admission, Villa Carlotta offers an elegant Neoclassical interior, Antonio Canova's famous *Maddalena Penitente* statue, and a garden (at its best in spring).

Cost and Hours: €9, daily April–mid-Oct 9:00-18:00, last 2 weeks of March and mid-Oct–mid-Nov 10:00-17:00, closed mid-Nov–mid-March, no photos inside the villa, tel. 034-440-405, www.villacarlotta.it.

Nearby: Tremezzo and **Cadenabbia** are pleasant lakeside resorts, each one an easy walk away. Boats serve both places (5-minute walk from either dock to the villa) and are reached by *traghetto* (ferry, dock in Cadenabbia) or the *battello* (slow boat, dock in Tremezzo).

To visit **Villa del Balbianello** (described next) after you see Villa Carlotta, catch the blue bus #C10 (turn right when exiting the villa and walk to the trash cans; bus departs at 10:50, 11:10, 11:58, 13:05, 13:57, 14:36, 15:06, and 15:36; €1.50, pay on bus). Get off at the second stop in Lenno, walk 30 yards, turn left, and follow the lakeside south to the lido of Lenno.

Villa del Balbianello

The dreamiest villa on the lake perches on a romantic promontory overlooking Lake Como and facing Bellagio. Built for a cardinal at the end of the 18th century on the remains of an old Franciscan church, the villa was the cardinal's palace of delights, where he could study and brainstorm with his friends. Today it reflects the exotic vision of its last owner, explorer Guido Monzino, who died in 1988—leaving his villa, his rich art collection, and mementos of his expeditions to the state. The upper floor serves as a museum of his expeditions, with memorabilia from his North Pole and Mount Everest adventures. The real masterpiece here is the terraced garden and elegant loggia, where the land fits the architecture and landscaping in a lovely way. This is a favorite choice for movie directors when they need a far-out villa to feature; scenes from *Casino Royale* and *Star Wars: Episode II* were filmed here.

Cost and Hours: Garden only-€7, garden with villa tour-€13, tours depart hourly Thu-Sun and Tue 10:00-18:00, closed Mon and Wed and mid-Nov-mid-March, tel. 034-456-110, www.fondoambiente.it.

Getting There: You can reach it on **foot** (on Tue and Sat-Sun only) by walking a half-mile from Lenno through the park. Otherwise, catch the more glamorous **speedboat shuttle** from Lido di Lenno (€5 one-way, €6 round-trip, Igor can also be hired for private tours, mobile 333-410-3854).

Isola Comacina

This remote little island, just south of Bellagio, offers peace, ancient church foundations, a small archaeological museum, swans, ducks, nice swimming, and a lovely view of Lake Como. It takes 30-45 minutes to walk around the island, but longer to savor it. Bring a picnic or try the snack bar at the dock.

Cost and Hours: €6, daily July-Aug 10:00-18:30, mid-March-June and Sept-Oct 10:00-17:00, closed Nov-mid-March, information at TI in mainland town of Ossuccio, tel. 034-456-369, www.isola-comacina.it, info@isola-comacina.it.

Getting There: The *isola* can be reached by ferry from Varenna (1 hour), Menaggio (50 minutes), or Bellagio (35 minutes). Look for trips to Isola Comacina (€5) on the Colico-Como *battello* schedule (listed in Lago di Como boat timetable, free at ticket booths at ferry docks). Check return times carefully (Como-Colico direction) and don't miss your boat. Usually only one trip a day each way works out for a visit. Allow about six hours, including travel time.

Como

On the southwest tip of the lake, Como has a good, traffic-free old town, an interesting Gothic/Renaissance cathedral, and a pleasant lakefront with a promenade (TI open Mon-Sat 9:00-13:00 & 14:00-17:00, closed Sun, tel. 031-269-712, www.lakecomo.it). It's an easy 10-minute walk from the boat dock to the train station (trains to Milan depart hourly, 30-90 minutes). Boats leave Como about hourly for mid-lake (ferries-€10, 2 hours, departures 7:35-16:45; hydrofoils-€15, 1 hour, departures 8:45-19:20, fewer on Sun; tel. 031-579-211, www.navigazionelaghi.it).

Sleeping in Como: For a cheap overnight, try the **$ Villa Olmo**

Hostel (€18 bunks, family room-€20.50/person, includes breakfast and sheets, €2/night extra for nonmembers, dinners-€5.50-12, pay guest computer, free Wi-Fi, laundry service available, baggage storage, free parking, bike rental, reception open 7:00-10:00 & 16:00-24:00, lockout 10:00-16:00, 24:00 curfew, closed mid-Nov-Feb, 20-minute walk from train station or dock, Via Bellinzona 2, tel. 031-573-800, www.ostellocomo.it, ostellocomo@tin.it).

All-Day Lugano Side-Trip

From Varenna or Bellagio, you can make a loop that lets you nip into Switzerland to see the elegant lake resort of Lugano, pass through the town of Como, and cruise a good part of Lake Como. Here's a good day plan: 9:00—ferry to Menaggio; 10:00—bus to Lugano (45 minutes, bring your passport); 11:30—explore Lugano, then train to Como (2/hour); 16:00—fast boat from Como to Varenna (departures also at about 17:00, 18:00, and 19:00). For information on Lugano, see www.ricksteves.com/lugano.

Lake Maggiore

Lake Maggiore is ringed by mountains, snowcapped in spring and fall, and lined with resort towns such as Stresa. While crassly touristic, Stresa is a handy base from which to explore the exotic garden islands of Lake Maggiore. And many consider it a pleasant last stop before flying home from nearby Malpensa Airport.

A visit to this region is worth the trouble for two islands, both with exotic gardens and lovely villas built by the Borromeo family. The Borromeos—through many generations since 1630—lovingly turned their islands into magical retreats, with elaborate villas and fragrant gardens. Isola Bella has a palace and terraced garden; Isola Madre has a villa and sprawling English-style (more casual) garden. A third island, Isola Superiore (a.k.a. Isola Pescatori), is simply small, serene, and residential. The Borromeos, who made their money from trade and banking, enjoyed the arts—from paintings (hung in lavish abundance throughout the palace and villa) to plays (performed in an open-air theater on Isola Bella) and marionette shows (you'll see the puppets that once performed here).

Tourists flock to the lakes in May and June, when flowers are in bloom, and in September. Concerts held in scenic settings draw music lovers, particularly during the summer Stresa Festival (get details from Stresa TI). For fewer crowds, visit in April, July, August (when Italians prefer the Mediterranean beaches), or October. In winter, the snow-covered mountains (with resorts a 1.5-hour drive away) attract skiers.

Planning Your Time

This region is best visited on a sunny day, when the mountains are clear, the lake is calm, and the heat of the sun brings out the scent of the blossoms. The two top islands for sightseeing are Isola Bella and Isola Madre. Isola Superiore has no sights, but is a peaceful place for lunch. You can stay the night in Stresa (accommodations listed later), but a day trip is sufficient for most.

Day Trip from Milan: Catch the one-hour, early train from Milan to Stresa (usually at 8:25, may require reservations; the next departure isn't until 11:25). Upon arrival in Stresa, walk 10 minutes downhill to the boat dock, and catch a boat to Isola Madre. Then work your way back to Isola Superiore for a lazy lunch, and on to Isola Bella for the afternoon, before returning to the town of Stresa and back to Milan.

Getting Around Lake Maggiore

Boats link the islands and Stresa, running about twice hourly. Allow roughly 10 minutes between stops. Since short round-trip hops add up fast (€7.80 each for Isola Bella and Isola Superiore, €10 for Isola Madre), it's best to simply buy the **all-day pass:** €10.10 for two islands (Bella and Superiore), or €16.90 for all the islands plus Pallanza (a town on the opposite shore) and Villa Taranto. An €18 **combo-ticket** combining the villas on Isola Bella and Isola Madre can be purchased at the boat dock (credit cards accepted).

Boats run daily April through September. The map on page 92 shows the route: Stresa, Carciano/Lido, Isola Bella, Isola Superiore, Baveno (lakeside town), Isola Madre, Pallanza, and Villa Taranto. This route is part of a longer one. To follow the boat schedule (free, available at boat docks, TI, and maybe your hotel), look at the Arona-Locarno timetable for trips from Stresa to the islands, and the Locarno-Arona timetable for the return trip to Stresa. Off-season, the boats cover a shorter route; check the timetable (public boat info: toll-free tel. 800-551-801, tel. 0322-233-200, www.navigazionelaghi.it, infomaggiore@navigazionelaghi.it).

Buy boat tickets directly from the dock ticket booth under the gallery to the left of the TI. Don't be fooled by the private taxi-boat drivers, most dressed in navy-blue uniforms and white hats (they look like Italian traffic cops); with their little sales booth on the sidewalk in front of the public boat launch, they'll try to talk you into paying way too much for private tours on their smaller boats.

Stresa

Stresa—which means "thin stretch"—was named for the original strip of fishermen's huts that lined the shore. Today, grand old hotels run along that same shore. The old town—basically a traffic-free touristy shopping mall—is just a few blocks deep, stretching inland from the main boat dock. A fine waterfront promenade leads past the venerable old hotels to the Lido (with the Carciano boat dock and a mountain cable car). Stresa's stately 19th-century lakeside hotels date back to the days when this town was on the "Grand Tour" circuit. In any Romantic-age resort like Stresa, hotels had names designed to appeal to Victorian aristocrats...like Palace (rather than Palazzo), Astoria, Bristol, and Victoria.

Nineteen-year-old Ernest Hemingway first came to Stresa in 1918. Wounded in Slovenia as an ambulance driver for the Italian Red Cross, he was taken to the Grand Hotel des Iles Borromees. This was the first hotel on the shore (from 1862), and it served—like its regal neighbors—as an infirmary during World War I. Hemingway returned to the same hotel in 1948, stayed in the same room (#205, now called the "Hemingway suite"—you can stay there for a couple of thousand dollars a night), and signed the guest book as "an old client." Another "old client" was Winston Churchill, who honeymooned here.

Orientation to Stresa

Tourist Information

The helpful TI, located to the right of the ticket window at the boat dock, has free maps and boat schedules (March-Oct daily 10:00-12:30 & 15:00-18:30; Nov-Feb Mon-Fri 10:00-12:30 & 15:00-18:30, Sat 10:00-12:30, closed Sun; Piazza Marconi 16, tel. 0323-30150, www.stresaturismo.it).

Helpful Hints

Internet Access: The **Newdata Internet Point** is a block off Piazza Cadorna in the old center (Mon-Sat 9:00-12:00 & 15:00-19:00, closed Sun, Via de Vit 15A, tel. 0323-30323, www.newdata.too.it).

Arrival in Stresa

At the train station, ask for a free city map at the newsstand (to the far right of the tracks as you exit the train). To get downtown, exit right from the station and take your first left (on Viale Duchessa di Genova). This takes you straight down to the lake (the boat dock is about four blocks to your right; ask for boat schedule at ticket window). The TI is next door on the same dock. Taxis charge a fixed rate of €8 for even the shortest ride in town.

Sights in Stresa

Islands and Gardens

▲▲Isola Bella

This island, nearest Stresa, has a formal garden and a fancy Baroque palace. Looking like a stepped pyramid from the water,

the island was named by Charles Borromeo (sponsor of Milan's Duomo) for his wife, Isabella. The island itself is touristy, with a gauntlet of souvenir stands and a corral of restaurants.

A few back streets provide evidence that people actually live here. While the Borromeo family now lives in Milan, they spend a few weeks on Isola Bella each summer (when their blue-and-red family flag flies from the top of the garden).

Cost and Hours: Palace and garden-€13, picture gallery-€3 extra, €18 combo-ticket includes the villa at Isola Madre (but not Isola Bella's picture gallery), daily late-March-late-Oct 9:00 18:00, closed late-Oct-late-March, last entry 30 minutes before closing, no photos in villa, tel. 0323-30556, www.borromeoturismo.it.

Audioguide: A fine €3 audioguide describes the palace, which also has posted English descriptions.

Services: A WC is at the garden entrance. Note that there are two docks on this island (one for each direction). Departure times are indicated by clocks at each dock. Picnicking is not allowed in the garden, but you can picnic at the point of the island (free and open to the public); take the black-and-white mosaic sidewalk to the left of the palace entrance.

Visiting the Island: Your visit is a one-way tour, starting with the palace and finishing with the garden. (There's no way to see the garden without the palace.) From the dock, head left to the huge palace, passing the public WCs.

In the lavishly decorated Baroque **palace,** stairs lead to stucco crests of Italy's top families (balls signify the Medici, bees mean the Barberini, and a unicorn symbolizes the Borromeos' motto: Humility). Here, you can choose to pay for a supplementary ticket to walk through the picture gallery (containing 130 beautifully restored 16th-century paintings from the Borromeo family's private collection, followed by an ornate throne room). Otherwise, continue right into the next room, where you'll see a portrait of the first Borromeo, and into a richly stuccoed grand hall, with an

80-foot-high dome and featuring an 18th-century model of the villa, including a grand entry that never materialized. The next room was the site of the 1935 Stresa Conference, in which Mussolini met with British and French diplomats in a united attempt to scare Germany out of starting World War II. Look for a copy of the treaty with Mussolini's signature on the wall next to the exit. Unfortunately, the "Stresa Front" soon fizzled when Mussolini attacked Ethiopia and joined forces with Hitler.

Next, Napoleon's bedroom comes with an engraving that depicts his 1797 visit (Napoleon is on a bench with his wife and sister enjoying festivities in his honor). The last rooms display souvenirs and gifts that the Borromeo family picked up over the generations.

Downstairs, many of the famous Borromeo marionettes are on display. (A larger collection is on Isola Madre.) The 18th-century grotto, decorated from ceiling to floor with shell motifs and black-and-white stones, still serves its original function of providing a cool refuge from Italy's heat. The dreamy marble statues are by Gaetano Monti, a student of Canova. Climbing out of the basement, look up at the unique cantilevered stairs; they're from a 16th-century fortress that predates this building.

Pass through the mirrored corridor and follow the path until you come to the ornate hall of 16th-century Flemish tapestries. This leads to the finale of this island visit: the beautiful **garden,** complete with Chinese white peacocks, which give it an exotic splash. Baroque—which is exactly what you see here—is all about controlling nature. Climb the stairs to see the terraced gardens, which are crowned by the Borromeo family unicorn. Back downstairs, follow the signs (hidden in the bushes) to the café/bookshop to get a 360-degree glimpse of the gardens. Then follow the signs to the exit. Gardeners continue on to the second exit to pass through Elisa's Greenhouse, named for Napoleon's sister and home to tropical plants.

▲Isola Superiore (Pescatori)

This sleepy island—home to 35 families—is the smallest and most residential of the three. It has a couple of good seafood restaurants, picnic benches, views, and, blissfully, nothing much to do—all under arbors of wisteria. A delight for photographers and painters, the island is never really crowded, except at lunchtime.

▲▲Isola Madre

Don't come here unless you intend to tour the sight, because that's all there is: an interesting furnished villa and a lovely garden filled with exotic birds and plants.

Cost and Hours: Villa and garden-€11, €18 combo-ticket includes Isola Bella, late-March-late-Oct daily 9:00-18:00, closed late-Oct-late-March, last entry 30 minutes before closing, no photos in villa, tel. 0323-31261, www.borromeoturismo.it.

Audioguide: A fine €3 audioguide is devoted almost entirely to the garden—a good investment to properly appreciate the plantings.

Services: A WC is next to the chapel. You'll also find a cafe/bookshop just outside the villa.

Visiting the Island: Visiting is a one-way affair. The sightseeing route is clearly signed, with a long stroll through the garden, villa, and chapel.

Eight gardeners (with the help of water continually pumped from the lake) keep this English-style **garden** paradise lush. It's a joy, even for those bored by flowers and foliage.

You'll see trees from around the world, and an exotic bird menagerie with golden and silver pheasants and Chinese peacocks. In front of the villa, a once-magnificent Himalayan cypress tree paints your world a streaky green. The 150-year-old tree, knocked down by a tornado in 2006 but successfully saved, is an attraction in its own right, with steel guy-wires now anchoring it firmly in place.

The 16th-century **villa** is the first of the Borromeo palaces. A century older than the Isola Bella villa, it's dark, somber, and dates from the Renaissance. The clever angled hinges keep the doors from flapping in the lake breeze. The family's huge collection of dolls, marionettes, and exquisite 17th-century marionette theater sets—painted by a famous La Scala opera set designer—fills several rooms. A corner room is painted to take you into an 18th-century Venetian Rococo sitting room under a floral greenhouse. Some of the garden's best flowers are in view immediately after leaving the villa.

Eating: While eating is best on Isola Superiore, Isola Madre has one eatery, **La Piratera Ristorante Bar** (€25 fixed-price tourist meal, daily 8:00-18:00, sit-down meals 12:00-15:30, simple sandwiches and slices of pizza to go anytime, picnic at rocky beach a minute's walk from restaurant, just to your right as you exit the gardens, tel. 0323-31171).

▲Villa Taranto Botanical Gardens

Garden lovers will enjoy this large landscaped park, located on the mainland a 10-minute boat ride beyond Isola Madre (across the lake from Stresa). The gardens are a Scotsman's labor of love. Starting in the 1930s, Neil McEacharn created this garden of delights—bringing in thousands of plants from all over the world—

LAKES

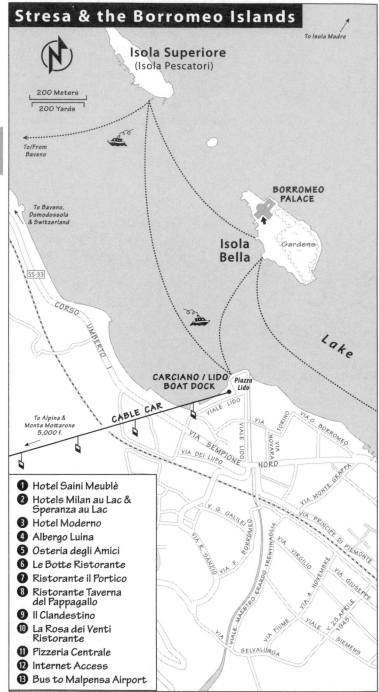

Stresa & the Borromeo Islands

To Isola Madre

Isola Superiore
(Isola Pescatori)

200 Meters
200 Yards

To/From
Baveno

To Baveno,
Domodossola
& Switzerland

SS-33

CORSO UMBERTO

BORROMEO PALACE

Isola Bella

Gardens

Lake

CARCIANO / LIDO
BOAT DOCK

Piazza
Lido

CABLE CAR

To Alpina &
Monte Mottarone
5,000 f.

VIALE LIDO

VIA SEMPIONE

VIALE LIDO

VIA DEI LUPO

NORD

VIA NOVARA

VIA TORINO

VIA G. BORROMEO

VIA MONTE GRAPPA

V. G. GALILEI

VIA PRINCIPE DI PIEMONTE

VIA R. SANZIO

VIA F. BORROMEO

VIALE MAESTRO ERARDO TRENTINAGLIA

VIA VIRGILIO

VIA 4. NOVEMBRE

VIA GIUSEPPE

VIA FIUME

VIALE V. 25 APRILE 1945

SIEMENS

SELVALUNGA

① Hotel Saini Meublè
② Hotels Milan au Lac & Speranza au Lac
③ Hotel Moderno
④ Albergo Luina
⑤ Osteria degli Amici
⑥ Le Botte Ristorante
⑦ Ristorante il Portico
⑧ Ristorante Taverna del Pappagallo
⑨ Il Clandestino
⑩ La Rosa dei Venti Ristorante
⑪ Pizzeria Centrale
⑫ Internet Access
⑬ Bus to Malpensa Airport

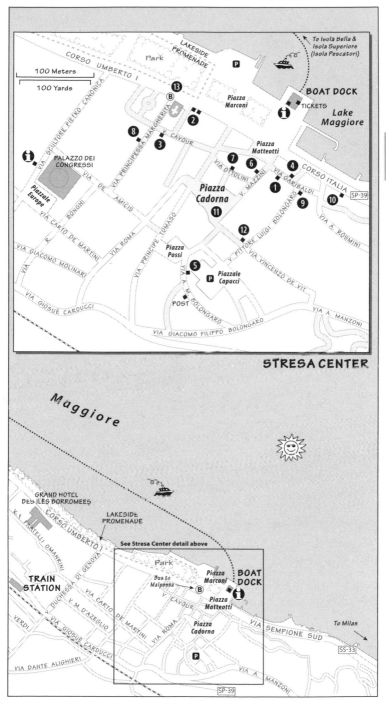

LAKES

STRESA CENTER

and here he stays, in the small mausoleum. The park's highlight is a terraced garden with a series of cascading pools. Villa Taranto is directly across the street from the boat dock.

Cost and Hours: €10, boat from Stresa-€12.40, daily mid-March-Oct 8:30-18:30, closed Nov-mid-March, tel. 0323-404-555, www.villataranto.it.

Mountain Cable Car

From Stresa's Lido, a cable car takes you up—in 2 stages and a 20-minute ride—to the top of Mount Mottarone (about 5,000 feet). From here, you get great views of neighboring peaks and, by taking a short hike, a bird's-eye view of the small, neighboring Lake Orta.

Cost and Hours: €18 round-trip, €11 one-way, daily 9:30-17:40 in summer, 8:10-17:20 in winter, 2-3/hour, bar midway up, tel. 0323-30295, www.stresa-mottarone.it.

Activities: To visit the **Alpine Gardens,** get off at the midway Alpina stop, where a 10-minute walk leads to the gardens (turn left as you leave; €3, April-Oct daily 9:30-18:00, closed Nov-March). The gardens come with great lake views and picnic spots, but can't compare to what you'll see on the islands.

If you plan to **hike** down, pick up the *Trekking Map* from the TI and allow four hours from the top of Mount Mottarone, or two hours from the Alpine Gardens.

You can rent a **bike** at the base of the cable-car lift (ask TI for details) and bring it on the cable car with you. It's a treacherous ride, enjoyable only for serious bikers. While the ride is nice on top, you'll fight traffic on congested, rough, and windy roads for the rest of the descent.

Day Trips from Stresa

▲Scenic Boat and Rail Trip to Locarno and Centovalli

This enjoyable all-day excursion from Stresa involves three segments. Before you embark on the trip, confirm all times, particularly the departure of the last boat from Locarno. Take the train from Stresa to Domodossola, then catch the "Centovalli" train for a 1.5-hour ride that links together remote mountain villages on your way to Locarno, in the Italian-speaking Swiss canton of Ticino (bring your passport). Spend an hour or so exploring this town, on the far end of Lake Maggiore. Then take the boat past loads of small lakeside hamlets back to Italy. As a relaxing finale, you'll cruise into your home port of Stresa. The trip can also be done in reverse (with the boat trip first). A special €32 "Lago Maggiore Express" ticket covers both the train and boat (purchase at the ferry dock in advance or email ahead of time if you want to eat on board; toll-free tel. 800-551-801, tel. 0322-233-200, www.lagomaggiore-express.com, infomaggiore@navigazionelaghi.it).

▲Lake Orta

Just on the other side of Mount Mottarone is the small lake of Orta. The lake's main town, Orta San Giulio, has a beautiful lakeside

piazza ringed by picturesque buildings. The piazza faces the lake with a view of Isola San Giulio. Taxi boats (€4 round-trip) make the five-minute trip throughout the day. The island is worth a look for the Church of San Giulio and the circular "path of silence," which takes about 10 minutes. In peak season, Orta is anything but silent, but off-season or early or late in the day, this place is full of peace and magic (TI open Sat-Sun 9:30-17:30, closed Mon-Fri, on Via Panoramica next to the parking lot downhill from the train station, tel. 0322-905-163).

Getting There: The train ride from Stresa to Orta-Miasino (a short walk from the lakeside piazza) takes 1.5-2 hours and requires a change or two (9/day). Public buses from Stresa's Piazza Marconi to Orta depart from near the TI (around €9 round-trip, 3/day mid-June–mid-Sept, confirm schedule at TI or at www.safduemila.com).

Sleeping in Stresa

Because Stresa's town is just a resort, I'd day-trip from Milan. But here are some good options if you'd like to stay.

$$ Hotel Saini Meublè is a cozy, 14-room place with rustic stonework and hardwood floors, located in a pedestrian zone a couple of blocks from the boat dock in the old center (Sb-€82, Db-€105, lower prices off-season, these rates promised to Rick Steves readers through 2014, elevator, guest computer and free Wi-Fi; Via Garibaldi 10, from Piazza Matteotti head up Via Mazzini and turn left on Via Garibaldi, tel. 0323-934-519, www.hotelsaini.it, info@hotelsaini.it). Gianni (Johnny) greets you at reception.

$$ Hotel Milan au Lac and its sister hotel next door, the yellow-brick **Speranza au Lac,** are impersonal four-star corporate-style hotels that cater mostly to tour groups, with 167 predictably comfortable rooms across from the boat dock (to the right as you leave the boat). Reception for both hotels is in Hotel Milan au Lac (Db-€125-160 depending on season and view, air-con, elevator, pay guest computer and Wi-Fi, laundry service, generally closed Nov-

March, Piazza Marconi 6/9, tel. 0323-31178, www.milansperanza. it, info@milansperanza.it).

$$ Hotel Moderno offers 54 peaceful and well-maintained pastel rooms on a pedestrian street a block from the main square (Sb-€98, Db-€150, discount for Rick Steves readers depending on availability, air-con, elevator, guest computer and free Wi-Fi, closed Nov-mid-March, Via Cavour 33; from the main square, with your back to the lake, find the church—hotel is behind the church on pedestrian street parallel to main road; tel. 0323-933-773, www.hms.it, moderno@hms.it).

$ Albergo Luina offers seven basic rooms above a restaurant (Sb-€62, Db-€95, breakfast-€4; 2 blocks off Piazza Matteotti—with back to lake, go left up small street; Via Garibaldi 21, tel. 0323-30285, luinastresa@yahoo.it, Cattia).

Eating in Stresa

Osteria degli Amici serves up tasty €10 risottos and pastas, with fast and friendly service under a canopy of grape and kiwi leaves (€7 wood-fired pizzas, daily 12:00-14:15 & 18:30-22:30, closed Wed Sept-June, deep in the old town past Piazza Cadorna at Via Bolongaro 33, tel. 0323-30453).

Le Botte offers a variety of Piedmont's regional specialties in a pub-grub casual atmosphere (€7-9 pastas, €9-15 *secondi,* daily 12:00-15:00 & 19:00-22:30 in summer, closed Thu Oct-March and all of Jan-Feb, Via Mazzini 6/8, tel. 0323-30462).

Ristorante il Portico is a cheerful, energetic place featuring several €16-26 multicourse tasting samplers and daily market specials on sidewalk tables or in their airy, fresh dining room. It's smart to reserve (piping-hot €6-10 pizzas, €7-10 pastas, €12-16 *secondi,* daily 12:00-16:00 & 19:00-24:00, closed off-season, Via Ottolini 9, tel. 0323-934-510).

Ristorante Taverna del Pappagallo is a bustling place with hardworking servers and happy locals. A glass case of desserts tempts you on the way in, but first try one of their shareable dishes, such as risotto with fish fresh from the lake, or their "moneybags" ravioli with pears and cheese (€6-10 pizzas, €7-10 pastas, €8-16 *secondi,* Thu-Tue 12:00-14:30 & 18:30-22:30, closed Wed, Via Principessa Marghertia 46, tel. 0323-30411).

Il Clandestino is a classy splurge. Lively Franco serves up creative fish and pasta dishes made with only the freshest ingredients (€15-18 pastas, €20 *secondi,* more expensive fixed-price menu available, Wed-Mon 19:15-23:00, Fri-Sun also 12:30-14:30, closed Tue, Via Rosmini 5, tel. 0323-30399).

La Rosa dei Venti, on the touristy main drag, has €5-8 pizzas and lakefront dining. They offer homemade pastas and creative risottos for €8-11 (big €8-10 salads, €14-19 *secondi*, daily 12:00-14:30 & 19:00-22:30, closed Tue off-season, 2 blocks south of the boat dock at Corso Italia 50, tel. 0323-31431).

The main square, **Piazza Cadorna,** is a carnival of residents selling things to tourists. Still, at night it has a certain charm. It seems anyone who claims to be a musician can get a gig singing for diners. **Pizzeria Centrale** (on a platform in the center) is a good place to enjoy the ambience. Their pizzas are decent, but don't order any serious food here.

Stresa Connections

From Stresa by Train to: Milan (about hourly, 1-hour fast train—but there can be gaps in service so check timetable carefully, 1.5-hour slow train), **Varenna** (roughly every two hours, 2.75-4 hours, transfer in Milan), **Venice** (7/day, 4-4.5 hours, transfer in Milan), **Domodossola** (near the Swiss border, almost hourly, 30 minutes).

To Malpensa Airport: For a **train-bus combination,** take the train toward Milan (departs hourly) and get off at Gallarate (after about 40 minutes), where cheap shuttle buses run to Malpensa's Terminal 1 (€2, pay driver, about 1-2/hour, 25 minutes). From Gallarate, the bus departs from the train station and runs 5:55-19:20; from Malpensa's Terminal 1, the bus runs 5:34-19:00 (tel. 0331 258-411, www.sea-aeroportimilano.it/en). For an early-morning flight, the first Stresa-Milan train departs at 5:45, connecting with Gallarate's second or third bus departure for Malpensa (confirm schedules locally).

Alibus Airport buses run between Stresa and Malpensa (€12, mid-April-Sept, 50 minutes; leaves Stresa from in front of the church next to Hotel Milan au Lac—near the ferry dock and TI at 6:30, 9:30, 11:30, 13:30, 16:30, and 19:30; leaves airport from bus stop 22 outside Terminal 1 at 8:30, 11:00, 13:30, 15:30, 18:30, and 21:00; confirm schedule, must reserve by 11:00 the previous day or by 11:00 Sat if booking for Sun or Mon bus—call 0323-552-172, book online at www.safduemila.com, or email alibus@safduemila.com).

Taxis to the airport cost €100 (1-5 people, €110 if traveling at night, 22:00-7:00) and take about an hour; your hotel can arrange the taxi for you, but will charge extra for booking it. It's easy to arrange a taxi on your own at the train station's taxi stand. Salvo Taxi is reliable (mobile 335-707-8894).

PRACTICALITIES

This section covers just the basics on traveling in Italy (for much more information, see *Rick Steves' Italy*). You can find free advice on specific topics at www.ricksteves.com/tips.

Money

Italy uses the euro currency: 1 euro (€) = about $1.30. To convert prices in euros to dollars, add about 30 percent: €20 = about $26, €50 = about $65. (Check www.oanda.com for the latest exchange rates.)

The standard way for travelers to get euros is to withdraw money from ATMs (which locals call a *bancomat*) using a debit or credit card, ideally with a Visa or MasterCard logo. Before departing, call your bank or credit-card company: Confirm that your card will work overseas, ask about international transaction fees, and alert them that you'll be making withdrawals in Europe. Also ask for the PIN number for your credit card in case it'll help you use Europe's "chip-and-PIN" payment machines (see below); allow time for your bank to mail your PIN to you. To keep your valuables safe while traveling, wear a money belt.

Dealing with "Chip and PIN": Much of Europe (including Italy) is adopting a "chip-and-PIN" system for credit cards, and some merchants rely on it exclusively. European chip-and-PIN cards are embedded with an electronic chip, in addition to the magnetic stripe used on our American-style cards. This means that your credit (and debit) card might not work at automated payment machines, such as those at train and subway stations, toll roads, parking garages, luggage lockers, and self-serve gas pumps. Memorizing your credit card's PIN lets you use it at some chip-and-PIN machines—just enter your PIN when prompted. If a payment machine won't take your card, look for a machine that takes cash or see if there's a cashier nearby who can process your transaction. The easiest solution is to pay for your purchases with cash you've withdrawn from an ATM using your debit card (Europe's ATMs still accept magnetic-stripe cards).

Phoning

Smart travelers use the telephone to reserve or reconfirm rooms, reserve restaurants, get directions, research transportation connections, confirm tour times, phone home, and lots more.

To call Italy from the US or Canada: Dial 011-39 and then the local number. (The 011 is our international access code, and 39 is Italy's country code.)

To call Italy from a European country: Dial 00-39 followed by the local number. (The 00 is Europe's international access code.)

To call within Italy: Just dial the local number.

To call from Italy to another country: Dial 00 followed by the country code (for example, 1 for the US or Canada), then the area code and number. If you're calling European countries whose phone numbers begin with 0, you'll usually have to omit that 0 when you dial.

Tips on Phoning: A mobile phone—whether an American one that works in Italy, or a European one you buy when you arrive—is handy, but can be pricey. If traveling with a smartphone, switch off data-roaming until you have free Wi-Fi. If you have a smartphone, you can use it to make free or inexpensive calls in Europe by using a calling app such as Skype or FaceTime when you're on Wi-Fi.

To make cheap international calls from any phone (even your hotel-room phone), you can buy an international phone card in Italy. These work with a scratch-to-reveal PIN code, allow you to call home to the US for pennies a minute, and also work for domestic calls.

Another option is buying an insertable phone card in Italy. These are usable only at pay phones, are reasonable for making calls within the country, and work for international calls as well (though not as cheaply as the international phone cards). Note that insertable phone cards—and most international phone cards—work only in the country where you buy them.

Calling from your hotel-room phone is usually expensive, unless you use an international phone card. For more on phoning, see www.ricksteves.com/phoning.

Making Hotel Reservations

To ensure the best value, I recommend reserving rooms in advance, particularly during peak season. Email the hotelier with the following key pieces of information: number and type of rooms;

From: rick@ricksteves.com
Sent: Today
To: info@hotelcentral.com
Subject: Reservation request for 19-22 July

Dear Hotel Central,

I would like to reserve a double room for 2 people for 3 nights, arriving 19 July and departing 22 July. If possible, I would like a quiet room with a bathroom inside the room.

Please let me know if you have a room available and the price.

Thank you!
Rick Steves

number of nights; date of arrival; date of departure; and any special requests. (For a sample form, see sidebar above.) Use the European style for writing dates: day/month/year. For example, for a two-night stay in July, you could request: "1 double room for 2 nights, arrive 16/07/14, depart 18/07/14." Hoteliers typically ask for your credit-card number as a deposit.

Given the economic downturn, hoteliers are often willing and eager to make a deal—try emailing several to ask their best price. In general, hotel prices can soften if you do any of the following: offer to pay cash, stay at least three nights, or mention this book. You can also try asking for a cheaper room or a discount, or offer to skip breakfast.

Eating

Italy offers a wide array of eateries. A *ristorante* is a formal restaurant, while a *trattoria* or *osteria* is usually more traditional and simpler (but can still be pricey). Italian "bars" are not taverns, but small cafés selling sandwiches, coffee, and other drinks. An *enoteca* is a wine bar with snacks and light meals. Take-away food from pizza shops and delis (such as a *rosticcería* or *tavola calda*) makes an easy picnic.

Italians eat dinner a bit later than we do; better restaurants start serving around 19:00. A full meal consists of an appetizer (antipasto), a first course (*primo piatto,* pasta, rice, or soup), and a second course (*secondo piatto,* expensive meat and fish/seafood dishes). Vegetables *(verdure)* may come with the *secondo*, but more often must be ordered separately as a side dish (*contorno*). Desserts (*dolci*) can be very tempting. The euros can add up in a hurry, but you don't have to order each course. My approach is to mix antipasti and *primi piatti* family-style with my dinner partners (skipping *secondi*). Or, for a basic value, look for a *menù del giorno*, a three- or four-course, fixed-price meal deal (avoid the cheapest ones, often called a *menù turistico*).

Good service is relaxed (slow to an American). You won't get the bill until you ask for it: *"Il conto?"* Most restaurants include a service charge in their prices (check the menu for *servizio incluso*—generally around 15 percent). To reward good service, add a euro or two for each person in your party. If you order at a counter rather than from waitstaff, there's no need to tip. Many (but not all) restaurants in Italy add a cover charge *(coperto)* of €1-3.50 per person to your bill.

At bars and cafés, getting a drink while standing at the bar *(banco)* is cheaper than drinking it at a table *(tavolo)* or sitting outside *(terrazza)*. This tiered pricing system is clearly posted on the wall. Sometimes you'll pay at a cash register, then take the receipt to another counter to claim your drink.

Transportation

By Train: In Italy, most travelers find it's cheapest simply to buy train tickets as they go. To see if a railpass could save you money, check www.ricksteves.com/rail. To research train schedules, visit Germany's excellent all-Europe website, www.bahn.com, or Italy's www.trenitalia.com. A private company called Italo is also running fast trains on major routes in Italy; see www.italotreno.it.

You can buy tickets at train stations (at the ticket window or at automated machines with English instructions) or from travel agencies. Before boarding the train, you must validate your train documents by stamping them in the machine near the platform (usually marked *convalida biglietti* or *vidimazione*). Strikes *(sciopero)* are common and generally announced in advance (but a few sporadic trains still run—ask around).

By Car: It's cheaper to arrange most car rentals from the US. For tips on your insurance options, see www.ricksteves.com/cdw, and for route planning, consult www.viamichelin.com. Theft insurance is mandatory in Italy ($15-20/day). Bring your driver's license. You're also technically required to have an International Driving Permit (sold at your local AAA office for $15 plus the cost of two passport-type photos; see www.aaa.com).

Italy's freeway *(autostrada)* system is slick and speedy, but you'll pay about a dollar for every 10 minutes of use. Be warned that car traffic is restricted in many city centers—don't drive or park in any area that has a sign reading *Zona Traffico Limitato* (*ZTL*, often shown above a red circle)...or you might be mailed a ticket later.

Local road etiquette is similar to that in the US. Ask your car-rental company about the rules of the road, or check the US State Department website (www.travel.state.gov, click on "International Travel," then specify your country of choice and click "Traffic Safety and Road Conditions").

A car is a worthless headache in cities—park it safely (get tips from your hotel). As break-ins are common, be sure all of your valuables are out of sight and locked in the trunk, or even better, with you or in your hotel room.

Helpful Hints

Emergency Help: For English-speaking **police** help, dial 113. To summon an **ambulance**, call 118. For passport problems, call the **US Embassy** (in Rome, 24-hour line—tel. 06-46741) or **US Consulates** (Milan—tel. 02-290-351, Florence—tel. 055-266-951, Naples—tel. 081-583-8111); or the **Canadian Embassy** (in Rome, tel. 06-854-441). For other concerns, get advice from your hotelier.

Theft or Loss: Italy has particularly hardworking pickpockets—wear a money belt. Assume beggars are pickpockets and any scuffle is simply a distraction by a team of thieves. If you stop for any commotion or show, put your hands in your pockets before someone else does.

To replace a passport, you'll need to go in person to an embassy or consulate (see above). Cancel and replace your credit and debit cards by calling these 24-hour US numbers collect: Visa—tel. 303/967-1096, MasterCard—tel. 636/722-7111, American Express—tel. 336/393-1111. File a police report either on the spot or within a day or two; you'll need it to submit an insurance claim for lost or stolen railpasses or travel gear, and it can help with replacing your passport or credit and debit cards. Precautionary measures can minimize the effects of loss—back up your digital photos and other files frequently. For more information, see www.ricksteves.com/help.

Time: Italy uses the 24-hour clock. It's the same through 12:00 noon, then keep going: 13:00, 14:00, and so on. Italy, like most of continental Europe, is six/nine hours ahead of the East/West Coasts of the US.

Business Hours: Many businesses have now adopted the government's recommended 8:00 to 14:00 workday (although in tourist areas, shops are open longer). Still, expect small towns and villages to be more or less shut tight during the midafternoon. Stores are also usually closed on Sunday, and often on Monday.

Sights: Opening and closing hours of sights can change unexpectedly; confirm the latest times with the local tourist information office or its website. Some major churches enforce a modest dress code (no bare shoulders or shorts) for everyone, even children.

Holidays and Festivals: Italy celebrates many holidays, which can close sights and attract crowds (book hotel rooms ahead). For information on holidays and festivals, check Italy's website: www.italia.it. For a simple list showing major—though not all—events, see www.ricksteves.com/festivals.

PRACTICALITIES

Numbers and Stumblers: What Americans call the second floor of a building is the first floor in Europe. Europeans write dates as day/month/year, so Christmas is 25/12/14. Commas are decimal points and vice versa—a dollar and a half is 1,50, and there are 5.280 feet in a mile. Italy uses the metric system: A kilogram is 2.2 pounds; a liter is about a quart; and a kilometer is six-tenths of a mile.

Resources from Rick Steves

This Snapshot guide is excerpted from my latest edition of *Rick Steves' Italy*, which is one of more than 30 titles in my series of guidebooks on European travel. I also produce a public television series, *Rick Steves' Europe*, and a public radio show, *Travel with Rick Steves*. My website, www.ricksteves.com, offers free travel information, a Graffiti Wall for travelers' comments, guidebook updates, my travel blog, an online travel store, and information on European railpasses and our tours of Europe. If you're bringing a mobile device on your trip, you can download free information from Rick Steves Audio Europe, featuring podcasts of my radio shows, free audio tours of major sights in Europe, and travel interviews about Italy (via www.ricksteves.com/audioeurope, iTunes, Google Play, or the Rick Steves Audio Europe free smartphone app). You can follow me on Facebook and Twitter.

Additional Resources

Tourist Information: www.italia.it
Passports and Red Tape: www.travel.state.gov
Travel Insurance Tips: www.ricksteves.com/insurance
Packing List: www.ricksteves.com/packlist
Cheap Flights: www.kayak.com
Airplane Carry-on Restrictions: www.tsa.gov/travelers
Updates for This Book: www.ricksteves.com/update

How Was Your Trip?

If you'd like to share your tips, concerns, and discoveries after using this book, please fill out the survey at www.ricksteves.com/feedback. Thanks in advance—it helps a lot.

PRACTICALITIES

Italian Survival Phrases

English	Italian	Pronunciation
Good day.	*Buon giorno.*	bwohn **jor**-noh
Do you speak English?	*Parla inglese?*	**par**-lah een-**glay**-zay
Yes. / No.	*Si. / No.*	see / noh
I (don't) understand.	*(Non) capisco.*	(nohn) kah-**pees**-koh
Please.	*Per favore.*	pehr fah-**voh**-ray
Thank you.	*Grazie.*	**graht**-seeay
You're welcome.	*Prego.*	**pray**-go
I'm sorry.	*Mi dispiace.*	mee dee-**speeah**-chay
Excuse me.	*Mi scusi.*	mee **skoo**-zee
(No) problem.	*(Non) c'è un problema.*	(nohn) cheh oon proh-**blay**-mah
Good.	*Va bene.*	vah **behn**-ay
Goodbye.	*Arrivederci.*	ah-ree-vay-**dehr**-chee
one / two	*uno / due*	**oo**-noh / **doo**-ay
three / four	*tre / quattro*	tray / **kwah**-troh
five / six	*cinque / sei*	**cheeng**-kway / **seh**ee
seven / eight	*sette / otto*	**seht**-tay / **ot**-toh
nine / ten	*nove / dieci*	**nov**-ay / **deeay**-chee
How much is it?	*Quanto costa?*	**kwahn**-toh **kos**-tah
Write it?	*Me lo scrive?*	may loh **skree**-vay
Is it free?	*È gratis?*	eh **grah**-tees
Is it included?	*È incluso?*	eh een-**kloo**-zoh
Where can I buy / find...?	*Dove posso comprare / trovare...?*	**doh**-vay **pos**-soh kohm-**prah**-ray / troh-**vah**-ray
I'd like / We'd like...	*Vorrei / Vorremmo...*	vor-**reh**ee / vor-**ray**-moh
...a room.	*...una camera.*	**oo**-nah **kah**-meh-rah
...a ticket to ____.	*...un biglietto per ____.*	oon beel-**yeht**-toh pehr
Is it possible?	*È possibile?*	eh poh-**see**-bee-lay
Where is...?	*Dov'è...?*	**doh**-veh
...the train station	*...la stazione*	lah staht-**seeoh**-nay
...the bus station	*...la stazione degli autobus*	lah staht-**seeoh**-nay **dayl**-yee **ow**-toh-boos
...tourist information	*...informazioni per turisti*	een-for-maht-**seeoh**-nee pehr too-**ree**-stee
...the toilet	*...la toilette*	lah twah-**leht**-tay
men	*uomini, signori*	**woh**-mee-nee, seen-**yoh**-ree
women	*donne, signore*	**don**-nay, seen-**yoh**-ray
left / right	*sinistra / destra*	see-**nee**-strah / **dehs**-trah
straight	*sempre diritto*	**sehm**-pray dee-**ree**-toh
When do you open / close?	*A che ora aprite / chiudete?*	ah kay **oh**-rah ah-**pree**-tay / keeoo-**day**-tay
At what time?	*A che ora?*	ah kay **oh**-rah
Just a moment.	*Un momento.*	oon moh-**mayn**-toh
now / soon / later	*adesso / presto / tardi*	ah-**dehs**-soh / **prehs**-toh / **tar**-dee
today / tomorrow	*oggi / domani*	**oh**-jee / doh-**mah**-nee

In an Italian-speaking Restaurant

English	Italian	Pronunciation
I'd like...	Vorrei...	vor-**rehee**
We'd like...	Vorremmo...	vor-**ray**-moh
...to reserve...	...prenotare...	pray-noh-**tah**-ray
...a table for one / two.	...un tavolo per uno / due.	oon **tah**-voh-loh pehr **oo**-noh / **doo**-ay
Non-smoking.	Non fumare.	nohn foo-**mah**-ray
Is this seat free?	È libero questo posto?	eh lee-bay-roh **kwehs**-toh **poh**-stoh
The menu (in English), please.	Il menù (in inglese), per favore.	eel may-**noo** (een een-**glay**-zay) pehr fah-**voh**-ray
service (not) included	servizio (non) incluso	sehr-**veet**-seeoh (nohn) een-**kloo**-zoh
cover charge	pane e coperto	**pah**-nay ay koh-**pehr**-toh
to go	da portar via	dah **por**-tar **vee**-ah
with / without	con / senza	kohn / **sehn**-sah
and / or	e / o	ay / oh
menu (of the day)	menù (del giorno)	may-**noo** (dayl **jor**-noh)
specialty of the house	specialità della casa	spay-chah-lee-**tah dehl**-lah **kah**-zah
first course (pasta, soup)	primo piatto	**pree**-moh peeah-toh
main course (meat, fish)	secondo piatto	say-**kohn**-doh peeah-toh
side dishes	contorni	kohn-**tor**-nee
bread	pane	**pah**-nay
cheese	formaggio	for-**mah**-joh
sandwich	panino	pah-**nee**-noh
soup	minestra, zuppa	mee-**nehs** trah, **tsoo**-pah
salad	insalata	een-sah-**lah**-tah
meat	carne	**kar**-nay
chicken	pollo	**poh**-loh
fish	pesce	**peh**-shay
seafood	frutti di mare	**froo**-tee dee **mah**-ray
fruit / vegetables	frutta / legumi	**froo**-tah / lay-**goo**-mee
dessert	dolci	**dohl**-chee
tap water	acqua del rubinetto	**ah**-kwah dayl roo-bee-**nay**-toh
mineral water	acqua minerale	**ah**-kwah mee-nay-**rah**-lay
milk	latte	**lah**-tay
(orange) juice	succo (d'arancia)	**soo**-koh (dah-**rahn**-chah)
coffee / tea	caffè / tè	kah-**feh** / teh
wine	vino	**vee**-noh
red / white	rosso / bianco	**roh**-soh / beeahn-koh
glass / bottle	bicchiere / bottiglia	bee-keeay-ray / boh-**teel**-yah
beer	birra	**bee**-rah
Cheers!	Cin cin!	cheen cheen
More. / Another.	Ancora un po.' / Un altro.	ahn-**koh**-rah oon poh / oon **ahl**-troh
The same.	Lo stesso.	loh **stehs**-soh
The bill, please.	Il conto, per favore.	eel **kohn**-toh pehr fah-**voh**-ray
tip	mancia	**mahn**-chah
Delicious!	Delizioso!	day-leet-seeoh-zoh

For more user-friendly Italian phrases, check out *Rick Steves' Italian Phrase Book & Dictionary* or *Rick Steves' French, Italian, and German Phrase Book.*

INDEX

INDEX

Audio Europe™

Rick's Free Travel App

Get your FREE **Rick Steves Audio Europe**™ app to enjoy...

- Dozens of self-guided tours of Europe's top museums, sights and historic walks

- Hundreds of tracks filled with cultural insights and sightseeing tips from Rick's radio interviews

- All organized into handy geographic playlists

- For iPhone, iPad, iPod Touch, Android

With Rick whispering in your ear, Europe gets even better.

Find out more at ricksteves.com

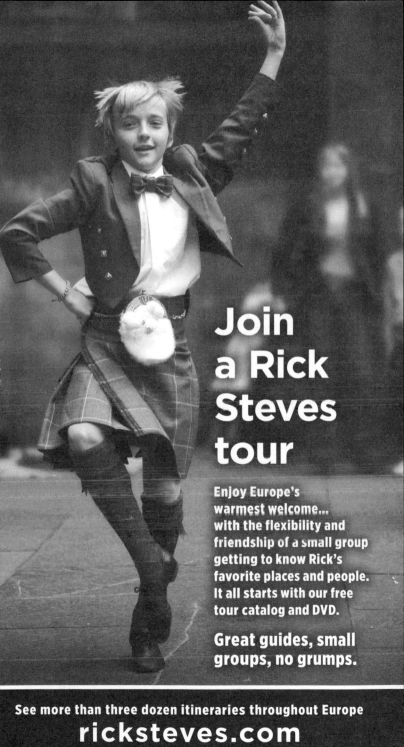

Start your trip at

Free information and great gear to

▶ Explore Europe

Browse thousands of articles, video clips, photos and radio interviews, plus find a wealth of money-saving tips for planning your dream trip. You'll find up-to-date information on Europe's best destinations, packing smart, getting around, finding rooms, staying healthy, avoiding scams and more.

▶ Travel News

Subscribe to our free Travel News e-newsletter, and get monthly updates from Rick on what's happening in Europe!

▶ Travel Forums

Learn, ask, share—our online community of savvy travelers is a great resource for first-time travelers to Europe, as well as seasoned pros.

Rick Steves' Europe Through the Back Door, Inc

ricksteves.com

turn your travel dreams into affordable reality

▶ Rick's Free Audio Europe™ App

The Rick Steves Audio Europe™ app brings history and art to life. Enjoy Rick's audio tours of Europe's top museums, sights and neighborhood walks—plus hundreds of tracks including travel tips and cultural insights from Rick's radio show—all organized into geographic playlists. Learn more at ricksteves.com.

▶ Great Gear from Rick's Travel Store

Pack light and right—on a budget—with Rick's custom-designed carry-on bags, wheeled bags, day packs, travel accessories, guidebooks, journals, maps and Blu-ray/DVDs of his TV shows.

130 Fourth Avenue North, PO Box 2009 • Edmonds, WA 98020 USA
Phone: (425) 771-8303 • Fax: (425) 771-0833 • ricksteves.com

Rick Steves

EUROPE GUIDES

Best of Europe
Eastern Europe
Europe Through the Back Door
Mediterranean Cruise Ports
Northern European Cruise Ports

COUNTRY GUIDES

Croatia & Slovenia
England
France
Germany
Great Britain
Ireland
Italy
Portugal
Scandinavia
Spain
Switzerland

CITY & REGIONAL GUIDES

Amsterdam, Bruges & Brussels
Barcelona
Budapest
Florence & Tuscany
Greece: Athens & the Peloponnese
Istanbul
London
Paris
Prague & the Czech Republic
Provence & the French Riviera
Rome
Venice
Vienna, Salzburg & Tirol

SNAPSHOT GUIDES

Berlin
Bruges & Brussels
Copenhagen & the Best of
    Denmark
Dublin
Dubrovnik
Hill Towns of Central Italy
Italy's Cinque Terre
Krakow, Warsaw & Gdansk
Lisbon
Madrid & Toledo
Milan & the Italian Lakes District
Munich, Bavaria & Salzburg
Naples & the Amalfi Coast
Northern Ireland
Norway
Scotland
Sevilla, Granada & Southern Spain
Stockholm

POCKET GUIDES

Amsterdam
Athens
Barcelona
Florence
London
Paris
Rome
Venice

Rick Steves guidebooks are published by Avalon Travel,
a member of the Perseus Books Group.

NOW AVAILABLE:
eBOOKS, DVD & BLU-RAY

TRAVEL CULTURE

Europe 101
European Christmas
Postcards from Europe
Travel as a Political Act

eBOOKS

*Nearly all Rick Steves guides
are available as eBooks. Check
with your favorite bookseller.*

RICK STEVES' EUROPE DVDs

11 New Shows 2013–2014
Austria & the Alps
Eastern Europe
England & Wales
European Christmas
European Travel Skills & Specials
France
Germany, BeNeLux & More
Greece, Turkey & Portugal
Iran
Ireland & Scotland
Italy's Cities
Italy's Countryside
Scandinavia
Spain
Travel Extras

BLU-RAY

Celtic Charms
Eastern Europe Favorites
European Christmas
Italy Through the Back Door
Mediterranean Mosaic
Surprising Cities of Europe

PHRASE BOOKS & DICTIONARIES

French
French, Italian & German
German
Italian
Portuguese
Spanish

JOURNALS

Rick Steves' Pocket Travel Journal
Rick Steves' Travel Journal

PLANNING MAPS

Britain, Ireland & London
Europe
France & Paris
Germany, Austria & Switzerland
Ireland
Italy
Spain & Portugal

Avalon Travel
a member of the Perseus Books Group
1700 Fourth Street
Berkeley, CA 94710

Printed in Canada by Friesens
Third printing July 2014

ISBN 978-1-61238-750-5

For the latest on Rick's lectures, guidebooks, tours, public radio show, and public television series, contact Europe Through the Back Door, Box 2009, Edmonds, WA 98020, tel. 425/771-8303, fax 425/771-0833, www.ricksteves.com, rick@ricksteves.com.

Europe Through the Back Door

Managing Editor: Risa Laib
Editorial & Production Manager: Jennifer Madison Davis
Editors: Glenn Eriksen, Tom Griffin, Cameron Hewitt, Suzanne Kotz, Cathy Lu, Carrie Shepherd, Gretchen Strauch
Editorial Assistant: Jessica Shaw
Editorial Intern: Alex Jacobs
Researchers: Ben Cameron, Cameron Hewitt, Helen Inman, Suzanne Kotz, Marijan Kriskovic, Cary Walker, Ian Watson
Maps & Graphics: David C. Hoerlein, Lauren Mills, Dawn Tessman Visser, Laura VanDeventer

Avalon Travel

Senior Editor and Series Manager: Madhu Prasher
Editor: Jamie Andrade
Associate Editor: Annette Kohl
Assistant Editor: Maggie Ryan
Copy Editor: Jennifer Malnick
Proofreader: Suzie Nasol
Indexer: Stephen Callahan
Cover Design: Kimberly Glyder Design
Maps & Graphics: Kat Bennett, Mike Morgenfeld

ABOUT THE AUTHOR

RICK STEVES

 Since 1973, Rick Steves has spent 100 days every year exploring Europe. Along with writing and researching a bestselling series of guidebooks, Rick produces a public television series *(Rick Steves' Europe)*, a public radio show *(Travel with Rick Steves)*, and an app and podcast *(Rick Steves Audio Europe);* writes a nationally syndicated newspaper column; organizes guided tours that take over ten thousand travelers to Europe annually; and offers an information-packed website (www.ricksteves.com). With the help of his hardworking staff of 80 at Europe Through the Back Door—in Edmonds, Washington, just north of Seattle—Rick's mission is to make European travel fun, affordable, and culturally enlightening for Americans.

Connect with Rick:

 facebook.com/RickSteves   twitter: @RickSteves